The One Necessary Thing

By

Dr. Norman Wise

Unedited Edition 1

Table of contents

Dedication

This book is dedicated to Kat Silverglate, Alisa Fisher, the "LORD's Lunch gang" and the small group that 'Beta Tested" this material and gave me helpful insights. I praise God for all of you!

Urgency of getting this book out in 2022 kept me from making all the changes that I should but I really felt it was important to put out a "unedited" first edition because of the message. So, I hope you can forgive the roughness of this copy and seek for the Lord to use it in your life.

Forward

Dr. Wise was one of my seminary professors. In my 50's and insecure about being in school again after decades away from exams and quizzes and surrounded by youngsters who knew all the latest technology and research methods, this teacher spoke like a friend sharing Jesus over a cup of coffee. His name – Wise – is profoundly fitting. Wisdom oozes out of him like honey from a comb. Whether the youngest or the oldest in the class, students found no pretense about him. They found a brother in Christ laid bare; a Jesus follower who wanted to share his love and knowledge with the spiritually hungry sitting at the feet of their teacher.

Most classes began with a lecture that quickly turned to a question that went like a wind where the Spirit led. No matter what we asked, Professor Wise went there. Without pause. Without objection. And without judgment. There were no stupid questions. There were only doorways that led again and again to "Messiah Jesus."

My minor edits to this work have been made with extreme care not to change the conversationally friend-to-friend flow and tone. It is, in my experience, that flow and tone which relaxes us to the point of hearing. I hear in these words penned by Professor Wise a man who has spent much time at the feet of Jesus' eaves dropping on His interaction with the disciples. The ones Jesus called "friend" because He took all he knew of the Father and He gave it to them. John 15:15.

Thank you Pastor Norm for giving what you know of the Father to so freely to so many. Thank you for speaking to us like friends.

Katherine "Kat" Silverglate, JD, MATS

It really began back in 1975 when for the first time I encountered John 15:1-8 as a living and real revelation to my heart. As a bible college student, I had read it many times before, but it had never "read me" till that day when suddenly the "wow" of what Jesus was actually saying struck me to the heart.

I had been striving to serve the LORD, experience spirituality, produce good works, make disciples, and be a faithful Christian since 1972 in a very focused and confused type of way.

As part of the "Jesus Movement" I had seen the Lord do a lot of things in and through me and my very imperfect witness of him in words and life. But I always felt something was lacking.

It was an exciting time, but also a puzzling time since exactly how to live for Christ was not clear to me. Sometimes, I felt that I was serving in my own strength to gain HIS approval. I was never sure if I had done enough to earn HIS approval even though I knew I was saved "by grace".

Then that day I read John 15:1-8, as if I had read it for the first time.

At that moment, I heard Jesus say through the passage, "Norm, I am the vine; you are the branch. Norm if you abide in me and I in you, Norm you will bear much fruit, for apart from me Norm you can do nothing." [John 15:5 ESV]

A spiritual lightbulb went off in my mind and heart. All I had to do was abide. Nothing more and nothing less. Whatever, this abiding experience was it was the key to everything.

Therefore, from that point on I sought to understand what it meant to "abide" and it is this quest that has led me to write this book so I can share with others some of the insights I have gained over the decades as I have sought to grow in my understanding of the "abiding experience."[1]

I consider myself to still be in the kindergarten of understanding "abiding" but have felt led to share my current understanding of "abiding" trusting the Lord will use it for some good in the lives of others.

My hope is that this book will be used like the "wardrobe" in the Chronicles of Narnia that will lead the reader into a new revelation of the life of Christ flowing into you and through you. It is not meant to be a commentary, though I will make comments on the scripture, but rather a bridge to a new experience of a more abundant experience of the abundant life we have been given by the Lord Jesus.

---

[1] Two key books that helped me in this process were True Spirituality by Francis Schaeffer and The Normal Christian Life by Watchmen Nee for those interested in some additional reading.

My prayer is that my reflections on John 15:1-8 may help you have your own personal eye-opening reality about the "abiding experience" so that in your life the LIFE of Christ Jesus will bear much bounty through YOU for the glory of the heavenly FATHER.   Amen

I believe in journaling as a process of meditation and change.   Therefore, this book is really a journaling book which will ask you to answer questions on what you have read and personalize the material carefully and prayerfully.

The most important part of this book is in the prayers it inspires you to pray, and the meditating caused by the journaling. Buy a journal now just to use with this book. Feel free to write notes on any blank spaced in the book, write out prayers, mark it up, and make the most use of it to be remembered and make an impact in your life!

So don't skip this part of it.   It is that process that I believe God will use to make this practical in your life.

It is better to just read one chapter a day and then journal on that chapter.   Slow is better.

I would also recommend that you read the chapter out loud so that you hear your voice actually say the words of each chapter. This will cause them to be more fully taken into your heart aa well as your mind,

You will notice a lot of repetition in this book. That is intentional.   Spaced repetition of truth is how our deepest parts of our souls and hearts change.   Don't fight the repetition but embrace it as a way to a deeper understanding of the presence of Christ Jesus in your life.

I am glad the Lord has led you to read and interact with this book   May it prove to be a blessing to your life.

I have printed this unedited version of the book because of the urgency I see in getting it out and the limited time I have to give to making some final edits which have been given to me by a couple very important people; Kat Silverglate and Alisa Fisher.   My hope is in 2023 to have an edited version which will include all their thoughts.

This work is written like a flowing stream. It is intended to wash over the hearer. To invite a pause and a restorative time in the living water. The truths contained here have become such a deep part of my life, I convey them more as I would precious truths to a friend sitting by my side than as a formally structured academic work. You will note that my personal reflections from my own brokenness appear at the end of some of the chapters. I share them as a fellow sojourner on the road with Christ. I share them so that you will know I join you on this journey as does every other Jesus follower who finds him or herself abiding or wanting to abide more.

Prayer

LORD, allow the readers of this book to see YOU more clearly, experience YOUR life in them, and overflow into the lives of others that abundant life YOU give to YOUR children. Amen

5 I am the vine; you are the branches. Whoever <u>abides</u> in me and I in him, he it is that bears much fruit, for apart from me you can do nothing. [John 15:5 ESV]

5 "I am the vine, you are the branches; the one who <u>remains</u> in Me, and I in him bears much fruit, for apart from Me you can do nothing. [John 15:5 NASB20]

<u>*Big idea of this book:*</u>

> <u>*To succeed at life I must abide in Jesus Christ and Jesus Christ must abide in me.*</u>

To the degree I abide in Jesus Christ I succeed. To the degree I fail to abide in Jesus Christ I fail.

If I totally fail to abide in Jesus Christ, then I totally fail at life.

> <u>Therefore, the most vital experience I need to seek in my life is to abide in Jesus Christ.</u>

I am writing this book for people who have come to the commitment and trust that Jesus of Nazareth is God the Son who became the Son of God, and is their personal Lord and Savior, who died to pay for their sins and rose again to demonstrate that HE paid in full the just penalty of their rebellion against God and is now their High Priest who is ready to help them in all of their times of struggle, temptation, pain, and need.

> *14 Therefore, since we have a great high priest who has passed through the heavens, Jesus the Son of God, let's hold firmly to our confession. 15 For we do not have a high priest who cannot sympathize with our weaknesses, but One who has been tempted in all things just as [we are, yet] without sin. 16 Therefore let's approach the throne of grace with confidence, so that we may receive mercy and find grace for help at the time of [our] need. [Heb 4:14-16 NASB20]*

The faith relationship you experienced when you first trusted in Jesus Christ as YOUR LORD and Savior was the beginning of an "abiding experience".

It is learning how to moment by moment to continue that experience of a faith relationship with Jesus Christ that is critical to living a successful Christian life.

6 And now, just as you accepted Christ Jesus as your Lord, you must continue to follow him. 7 Let your roots grow down into him, and let your lives be built on him. Then your faith will grow strong in the truth you were taught, and you will overflow with thankfulness. [Col 2:6-7 NLT]

This book will attempt to explain how we can explore and seek to have this moment-by-moment faith experience in our lives daily in a practical way.

Now, if you have not yet come to accept Jesus Christ as YOUR personal Lord and Savior that would be the first step in experiencing what the Lord Jesus calls an "abiding" or "remaining" relationship with HIM which is vital to you not wasting your life.

Therefore, I would urge you to take the next 21 days and read one chapter of the gospel of John since it was written by Jesus' best friend to help people to come to this vital first step of trusting in Christ Jesus to become the most important person in your life.

Even if you know Jesus as your Lord and Savior but have never read the gospel of John that would be a great activity for you to do over the next 21 day.[2] You can get a study guide on how to do this through the Pocket Testament League at their website. https://www.ptl.org/lp/en-21dc/

30 Now Jesus did many other signs in the presence of the disciples, which are not written in this book (the gospel of John); 31 but these are written so that you may believe that Jesus is the Christ, the Son of God, and that by believing you may have life in his name. [Jhn 20:30-31 ESV)

I would also recommend you watch the 2017 movie "A Case For Christ" which tells the story of Lee Strobel, an investigative reporter for the Chicago Tribune who was an atheist who came to both intellectual conviction that Jesus was not a lunatic or liar, but actually LORD as he claimed and began to have an "abiding" personal relationship with the Living Jesus Christ as well.

The book <u>More Than A Carpenter by Josh McDowell</u> I have also found helpful in becoming convinced that Jesus of Nazareth is in fact Lord and Savior.

It is vital that we have firm intellectual faith in the truthfulness of the claims of Jesus Christ for us to have a real "abiding relationship" with him. Our minds as well as our hearts must embrace Jesus Christ in order to have a true abiding faith in HIM.

As a person who had to have these intellectual issues settled before I could have a stable relationship with Jesus Christ, I want to assure you I firmly believe that if you seek to find the truth you will find that Jesus is the TRUTH. Christ Jesus is not afraid of a doubting Thomas.

25 So the other disciples told him, "We have seen the Lord." But he said to them, "Unless I see in his hands the mark of the nails, and place my finger into the mark of the nails, and place my hand into his side, I will never believe." 26 Eight days later, his disciples were inside again, and Thomas was with them. Although the doors were locked, Jesus came and stood among them and said, "Peace be with you." 27 Then he said to Thomas, "Put your finger here, and see my hands; and put out your hand, and place it in my side. Do not disbelieve, but believe." 28 Thomas answered him, "My Lord and my God!" 29 Jesus said to him, "Have you believed because you have seen me? Blessed are those who have not seen and yet have believed." [Jhn 20:25-29 ESV]

---

[2] Here is a 21 day challenge that can help you gain the most from reading the gospel of John provided by the Pocket Testament League. https://www.ptl.org/lp/en-21dc/

Leonard Sweet helps us to understand what we are talking about here when he writes: "So, what is Christianity? It is Christ. Nothing more. Nothing less. Christianity is not an ideology or a philosophy. Neither is it a new type of morality, social ethic, or worldview. _Christianity is the "good news" that beauty, truth, and goodness are found in a person._ And true humanity and community are founded on and <u>experienced by connection to that person</u>. Conversion is more than a change in direction; <u>it's a change in connection</u>.[3]"

I would say that Christianity has within it an ideology, a philosophy, a new type of morality, a social ethic and worldview.   However, one can understand all those things and yet miss the heart of the faith which is to have a personal and real connection with Christ Jesus in a personal relationship. Without that "real connection" then we really don't understand anything about having faith in Christ Jesus at all.

Journal moment – How is a change of direction different than a change in connection? Why is this important?

---

[3] Sweet, Leonard; Viola, Frank. Jesus Manifesto: Restoring the Supremacy and Sovereignty of Jesus Christ (Kindle Locations 204-208). Thomas Nelson. Kindle Edition. – I would modify this to "not only an ideology, or a philosophy, or world view" since Christianity is all of these things and yet so much more at core a relationship with Christ Jesus.

This "connection" is a real abiding relationship with the person of Jesus Christ.

Therefore, wherever you are at in your faith journey you are welcome to begin to explore having this vital "abiding" relationship with Jesus Christ.

This is so vital an experience that Christ Jesus says that if it occurs in our lives we will be "fruitful" and effective in producing lives that give glory to God the Father, but if we don't abide, we will be powerless to live effectively.

To make this connection with Christ Jesus you only need to sincerely call out to HIM in prayer. You may want to pray a prayer like this to begin YOUR "abiding experience" with the Lord Jesus.

> *"LORD Jesus, I believe you died on the cross to pay for my sins and are alive today being physically raised from the dead to provide me the forgiveness of my immoral actions, and a new abundant life connected with YOU and having YOUR life in me. So now come into my life LORD Jesus and bring me YOUR salvation, strength, and wisdom. I want YOU to live in union and communion with me. Amen"*

Even if you feel you have accepted the Lord saying a prayer like this today is not a bad idea. Our "abiding" in Christ is really our moment by moment accepting, trusting, and believing in a fresh way every second of our lives. The Christian lives by faith in Christ Jesus over and over again.

Clearly once I have asked Jesus Christ to abide in my life, then learning how to practically experience the abiding presence and life of Christ Jesus in my life must become the highest priority of my life.

That is what this book will explore so that you can daily bear much fruit for so that your life will honor the Father's love shown to us in Christ Jesus. This life of Jesus Christ pouring out divine love through you will be the fulfillment of all you were created to accomplish in your life!

Journaling on Preface and Introduction

What made the most impact on you as your read the Preface and Introduction?

Why do you think this impacted you?

What was confusing or unclear to you?

What questions do you have at this point in seeking to learn about the "abiding experience"

How did you come to accept Jesus Christ as your Lord and Savior. Write out your testimony of how you came to know the Lord Jesus?

Describe your life before you came to know Jesus as YOUR Savior.

What circumstances, people, experiences, and verses helped you to accept Jesus as your Savior?

What changes have come into your life as a person who has come into trusting in the Lord Jesus to forgive your sins and guide you in your life?

Have you shared your testimony with others?   Would there be someone in your life that would be helped by knowing how you came to have a personal relationship with Jesus?

Personal Journal on preface and Introduction. -   I have spent more time thinking, pondering, meditating, and processing in preparation for the writing of this book than any other I have written up to this point.   It is a topic that has dominated my life for decades and which I am drawn back to over and over again.   John 15:1-8 is a passage that impacts my life daily. My hope is that you will begin to hear this passage in a new way and from that new perspective on the passage gain a deeper awareness of how Christ Jesus is in you and transforming you from the inside out.

Sometimes the best way to understand an idea or experience in through a story.

This story of two sisters is one that for me gets to the very heart of what it means to "abide" in our Christian lives.

The Story of Martha and Mary

38 As Jesus and his disciples were on their way, he came to a village where a woman named Martha opened her home to him. 39 She had a sister called Mary, who sat at the Lord's feet listening to what he said. 40 But Martha was distracted by all the preparations that had to be made. She came to him and asked, "Lord, don't you care that my sister has left me to do the work by myself? Tell her to help me!"

41 "Martha, Martha," the Lord answered, "you are worried and upset about many things, 42 but few things are needed—or indeed only one. c Mary has chosen what is better, and it will not be taken away from her." Luke 10:38-42

We live in a world that many times evaluates us by our performance. Because of this, we can be sympathetic to Martha in this story.   She is doing the practical things that need to be done and that makes the most sense to us.   She is a hard worker. It is easy for us to respect that virtue in her life.

Christ Jesus had come to her house. No greater honor could come to anyone. Everyone should do all they could to prepare a great meal and make everything perfect during the LORD's visit.

There was much to do" for the Lord."

Yet, amid all this need to work to do thing "for the Lord", Mary simply stopped to sit at Jesus' feet and listen to HIS words. What did this mean? Why was it important?

This seemingly objective statement is actually the description of a model disciple in Judaism. "Sitting at one's feet" is a classic description of a rabbinic disciple (2 Kgs 4:38; 6:1; Acts 22:3; m. ʾAbot. 1:4). In Luke, "sitting" (or "falling") at Jesus' feet symbolizes faith (8:41).   James R. Edwards, The Gospel according to Luke,

---

Mary defined herself, saw herself, and been chosen by the Lord Jesus to be HIS disciple. Jesus accepted her taking the place of a disciple at HIS feet and she knew that was where she belonged. Her identity as a believing disciple made her "sitting "at HIS feet as natural as breathing. She did not see herself doing a "good thing" but receiving "the best thing" by being absorbed in deep fellowship with the Lord.

How could she do this?   Didn't she see how much had to be done? Didn't she want to "do things" for the Lord?

Yet what has happened is Mary is fully absorbed with the presence and person of the LORD Jesus Himself and for her that is the only thing that is important.

Martha of course even doubted the Lord at this point.   How could HE reward such "laziness"?

Martha felt Jesus Christ did not care that an injustice was occurring. In doing things "for the Lord" she came to doubt if the Lord cared about her.   She also failed to become absorbed by the person of the LORD but only cared about doing things "for HIM."

Mary was treating her in an unfair way, making her do all the work. Why did the Lord Jesus not rebuke her?   While working "for the Lord", she started to doubt the fairness of the Lord.

Yet it is here the Lord gives her a reality check.   He does so with kindness and grace.   Saying her name twice was a way of expressing affection and care for a person in that culture.

His tone was gentle, supportive, sympathetic, understanding, and compassionate. He was not angry with her. She was also a disciple just like Mary was a disciple.

The Lord Jesus said there always will be things to do, but only one thing is necessary, vital, and supremely important. That is simply "being" with HIM. Believing in HIM, absorbed by HIM, remaining with HIM, and listening to HIM. Personal relationship with HIM is the one essential thing!

To simply be with Christ Jesus was vital. Gaining from HIM life, light, wisdom, and HIS presence. This is the only thing that really matters in the end. Without this nothing else really matters. That is a wild and radical claim to make. But the Lord Jesus makes such a claim here.

Fellowship with Christ Jesus, is so vital that no amount of being busy for the LORD could ever replace that connection with HIM.

If Martha and Mary had both just sat at HIS feet, there may have been a delay in the meal being prepared or perhaps there would have been a day of fasting, but Martha would have had a better understanding of the LORD and not have felt out of touch with HIS heart.

This same lesson is hard for us to learn.

The LORD Jesus reinforces this truth in John 15, and we are going to spend some time now meditating on this spiritual reality of life.

That the one thing that is necessary, vital, and of ultimate importance; is simply being in a focused, friendly, and firmly loyal relationship with Christ Jesus This is the key to the "abiding experience".

To abide is to sit at the feet of Jesus and want to soak in HIS presence, power, and peace. To sit and listen to HIS WORD to us and for us.   This is what it means to abide.

Prayer: Lord Jesus, it is so easy for me to be like Martha. There are so many things that need to be done for YOU.   How can I spend time just being with YOU when so many tasks need to be done? They are important, practical, and needed.   Yet, Lord, you tell me there is one truly necessary thing that must be done. I must stop, sit, and be with YOU for without YOU I can do nothing worth doing. This is much harder than working hard for YOU. Stopping is not easy.   Help me to know that without pausing to be with YOU, nothing I do will really matters. Amen

Note for Martha: What you do is vital. Many things will have to be done. But learning to first spend time with the LORD and then while enjoying the fruit of that fellowship taking up the tasks is a better approach. I think that in the context there would have been a time for Mary to help Martha, but first she wanted to soak in as much time with the Lord as she could.   Yes, there is work to be done in the strength of the LORD and it flows from having fellowship with Jesus.

Journaling Questions

1. Why does Martha seem right in this story? Have you ever been like Martha busy doing the work of the Lord but not having time to know the Lord personally?

2. What makes Mary look selfish? Do you feel selfish if you just stop to spend time with the Lord? Do you ever stop to spend time with the Lord?

3. How could you in your life stop and simply spend time with the Lord Jesus? How would this look for you? What experiences in your life have been times when you felt most intimate with the Lord?

4. What hinders you from doing this more often?

Personal Journal on Chapter One - I have found there has been always a tension between the "Martha spirit" and the "Mary spirit" in me. I have been guilty of being a "kingdom workaholic" filling my schedule with important tasks and ministry. At times as a businessman I also lost the "life balance" needed to have a healthy mental, emotional, and relational life. Yet, each time the LORD in HIS grace called me back to seeing the essential need I had of making my relationship with HIM and "sitting at HIS feet" the most essential aspect of my schedule and life. The truth of this passage is one that I have had to process through many times in order to keep my priorities straight.

We are going to look at John 15:1-8 hoping from a study of it we will experience abiding in Christ Jesus and live more fruitful, useful, and effective lives which brings honor to our heavenly Father.

It is one of the most important teachings of the Lord Jesus. In fact, if we can experience what Jesus Christ teaches in this portion of scriptures then we will live successful and effective lives for God. Success is found in having a believing personal relationship with the LORD. To have that connection is to succeed in why we have been created.   To know HIM is the purpose of our lives.

Our first step will be to get a clear intellectual overview of John 15:1-8.

Let us try to understand how these eight verses are organized

1 "I am the true vine, and My Father is the vinedresser. 2 "Every branch in Me that does not bear fruit, He takes away; and every [branch] that bears fruit, He prunes it so that it may bear more fruit. 3 "You are already clean because of the word which I have spoken to you.

4 "Abide in Me, and I in you. As the branch cannot bear fruit of itself unless it abides in the vine, so neither [can] you unless you abide in Me.

5 "I am the vine, you are the branches; he who abides in Me and I in him, he bears much fruit, for apart from Me you can do nothing.

6 "If anyone does not abide in Me, he is thrown away as a branch and dries up; and they gather them and cast them into the fire, and they are burned.

7 "If you abide in Me, and My words abide in you, ask whatever you wish, and it will be done for you. 8 "My Father is glorified by this, that you bear much fruit, and [so] prove to be My disciples. [John 15:1-8 NASB]

Basic Structure of John 15:1-8

It is always helpful when looking at the passage that we see the literary structure of what we are reading so we can get a clear outline of it in our mind and hearts.

1. VS. 1-3 – I am the vine and you are the branches - Teaching
2. Vs. 4 – Abide in me - Command
3. Vs. 5 – I am the vine and you are the branches - Teaching

Negative warning Vs 6 – If there is no abiding there is no life or fruit.

Positive promise Vs 7-8 – If you do abide there will fruit, the FATHER will be glorified

<u>We see that the main point here is to learn to "abide in Jesus" and that without that there is no effective living or fruit; but with that we will be effective and bring glory to God the Father.</u>

This teaching clearly states that success or failure all rests on experiencing this one reality, which is "abiding".   This an experience we are commanded to seek and realize.

Two Key Words

This passage has two key words that need to be defined.

One is Abide.   What does Christ Jesus mean when He commands us to "abide" in HIM?

The Greek word is "Meno" and is translated as "abide" or "remain". It can mean to "sojourn" with someone on a trip. To stay with someone in a fixed relationship.

It is by faith in Jesus Christ that we become connected to HIM and have "received" HIM into our lives.   This begins our "abiding with HIM and HIS abiding with us.

12 But as many as received Him, to them He gave the right to become children of God, [even] to those who believe in His name, [John 1:12 NASB95]

To abide means to moment by moment be in a living relationship of faith with the person of Christ Jesus.

The Christian will live by faith in Christ Jesus moment by moment.   The stronger the faith in Christ Jesus the greater the flow of Christ's life through the believing disciple.   The greater the faith in Christ Jesus the deeper and more profound the "abiding experience".

"Here is a mutual abiding or indwelling. The life-principle circulates through the branches, just as they perpetuate the living connection between the branch and the center of the life. The mutual relations show that human nature is in infinite need, and, apart from the new life-principle, will perish. The abiding of the branch in the vine suggests the continuance of vital connection' with the living stem, and supposes that connection kept up by constant faith, so that the believer is in a position to draw life from the legitimate source. The abiding of the vine in the branch - "I in you" -is the perpetual inflow into the subordinate life, of the living grace which makes the believer's life one with his Lord's. As he said (John 14:19), "Because I live, and ye shall live;" so now, As the branch cannot bear fruit from itself - from its own inherent vitality - except it abide in the vine - except this connection is maintained - in like manner no more (or, so neither) can ye, except ye abide in me. "(Pulpit Commentary on John 15:4)

What is it to have faith in Christ Jesus?

It is to <u>trust</u> in HIM as the ultimate <u>revelation</u> and PROPHET, the very incarnation of TRUTH. It is to <u>rely</u> on HIM as the ultimate <u>redeemer</u> and High PRIEST who has by HIS sacrifice on the cross paid in full the just punishment of all my moral failures, and it is to <u>receive</u> HIM as the ultimate <u>ruler</u> and PRINCE who provides, protects, and guides me in my daily life.

(Journal exercise – Stop reading and paraphrase the paragraph above in your own words)

None of us totally believes, trusts, relies upon, or receives Christ Jesus as we should but at various times our faith is greater or diminishes.

Based on the strength of this faith will determine just how much the "fruit" of Jesus Christ flows out of us.

Even our faith is a gift of God that comes to us through a revelation of Jesus Christ.

17 So faith [comes] from hearing, and hearing by the word of Christ. [Romans 10:17 NASB95]

The Holy Spirit uses the preaching and remembrance of Christ Jesus to produce in us true faith in HIM.

Therefore, if I lack faith, I need to pursue hearing more about the LORD Jesus and <u>preach the gospel to myself</u> so that my trust, reliance, and acceptance of HIM will grow stronger moment by moment and day by day.

This process will be fulfilled when "faith" gives way to "seeing" which then allows us to become totally transformed into the likeness of Jesus Christ.

1 See how great a love the Father has bestowed on us, that we would be called children of God; and [such] we are. For this reason the world does not know us, because it did not know Him. 2 Beloved, now we are children of God, and it has not appeared as yet what we will be. We know that when He appears, we will be like Him, because we will see Him just as He is. 3 And everyone who has this hope [fixed] on Him purifies himself, just as He is pure. [1John 3:1-3 NASB95]

When we see Christ Jesus face to face in the ultimate revelation of HIS appearing, this experience of "total faith" will immediately transform us into the moral perfection of Jesus Christ.   As David Mathis of Desiring God ministries writes.

"Blessed are the pure in heart, for they shall see God. —Matthew 5:8

"What will it mean, in the end, to see God? This longing, knit deep into the fabric of our being, is at once one of Scripture's great promises and puzzles.

In the Beatitudes, Christ himself pledges this greatest of all sights to the pure in heart (Matthew 5:8). Among the most famous lines penned by the apostle Paul, we have, "For now we see in a mirror dimly, but then face to face" (1 Corinthians 13:12). Hebrews tells of a "holiness without which no one will see the Lord" (Hebrews 12:14). And in the final chapter of holy writ, the Apocalypse promises of the people of God, "They will see his face" (Revelation 22:4).

Christians have long called this great promise "the beatific vision," meaning "the sight that makes happy." As creatures who seek happiness, this is the great Happiness to come, the moment when we, at last, stand face to face before our God to perceive him visually and immediately and more."[4]

When we experience the "beatific vision" we will perfectly reflect HIM into the world and become just like HIM in HIS humanity in every way when we see Jesus Christ, face to face.   Such perfection will not be ours as long as we "see in a mirror darkly" (1 Corinthians 13:12) but due to the joyful anticipation of this being accomplished when we "see HIM", we strive to purify ourselves as HE is pure by walking more and more by faith daily.

To abide means to remain in a state of true faith in Christ Jesus which establishes a transforming relationship with HIM in our lives and allows HIM to bear His "fruit" in us.

The second word that needs to be defined is "fruit".

But what is the "fruit" of Christ?

It would seem clear that the "fruit" of Christ is LOVE.

34 "A new commandment I give to you, that you love one another, even as I have loved you, that you also love one another. 35 "By this all men will know that you are My disciples, if you have love for one another." [Jhn 13:34-35 NASB95]

6 For in Christ Jesus neither circumcision nor uncircumcision means anything, but faith working through love. [Gal 5:6 NASB95]

To love well is to live well.   All the commands of God can be reduced to LOVE.

36 "Teacher, which is the great commandment in the Law?" 37 And He said to him, " 'YOU SHALL LOVE THE LORD YOUR GOD WITH ALL YOUR HEART, AND WITH ALL YOUR SOUL, AND WITH ALL YOUR MIND.' 38 "This is the great and foremost commandment. 39 "The second is like it, 'YOU SHALL LOVE YOUR NEIGHBOR AS YOURSELF.' 40 "On these two commandments depend the whole Law and the Prophets." [Mat 22:36-40 NASB95]

But how can we love unconditionally and sacrificially as Christ Jesus loved us?

<u>This is not an act of the will</u> but the fruit of the Holy Spirit active in our lives.

16 But I say, walk by the Spirit, and you will not carry out the desire of the flesh. ... 22 But the fruit of the Spirit is love, joy, peace, patience, kindness, goodness, faithfulness, 23 gentleness, self-control; against such things there is no law. 24 Now those who belong to Christ Jesus have crucified the flesh with its passions and desires. 25 If we live by the Spirit, let us also walk by the Spirit. [Gal 5:16, 22-25 NASB95]

---

[4] https://www.desiringgod.org/articles/we-will-see-his-face

Notice that the "fruit" of the Spirit is singular not plural.   The "fruit" is love!

The "fruit" is love manifested as joy, love manifested as peace, love manifested as patience, love manifested as kindness, love manifested as goodness, love manifested as faithfulness, loave manifested as gentleness, and love manifested as self-control.

To bear the fruit of the Holy Spirit comes by us experiencing an abiding or remaining in a true faith relationship with the Living Christ and HIS LOVE overflowing out of us into all our relationships and actions.

Movement by moment personal faith in Christ Jesus, leads to HIS life being poured into me through the Holy Spirit, and this manifest itself through me as words, actions, and attitudes of DIVINE LOVE.

As I see the Lord Jesus more clearly by faith, I love HIM more dearly, and then follow HIM more nearly in all my behavior, moment by moment and day by day. This is the pattern of living a "normal" Christian life. The greater my faith in Christ Jesus the greater my bearing of fruit will occur.

Prayer: LORD Jesus thank YOU for abiding and remaining with me and in me each moment and allow me by trust and dependence on YOU abide and remain in YOU as a normal way of living my daily life. Help the consistency and intensity of me, by faith abiding in YOU to increase. Spirit of the Living Christ now bear YOUR fruit of LOVE in me and overflow out of me into every relationship in my life. Incarnate in me YOUR LOVE so that the Father in heaven will be glorified as people see YOUR LOVE flow out of me.   Amen

Journal on Chapter Two – Day Two

1. Paraphrase in your own words John 15:1-8

2. What is the "Big Idea" that Jesus Christ is teaching in John 15:1-8

3. What is the most practical insight you gained by reading this chapter?   How could you apply this chapter to your personal life.?

4. What puzzles you still about abiding?

5. Art Journaling – Draw a picture of a vine, branches, and fruit. Label the fruit with the fruit of the Spirit. Ask the Lord to take this drawing as a way to help your heart focus on the reality of all of our life has to be an overflow of HIS life in us.

Examples of this type of art

https://www.pinterest.com/pin/454722893622527573/

https://www.pinterest.com/pin/546413367291125136/

Personal Journal on Chapter Two - The first time that I was taught John 15:1-8 in Bible College the idea of the "Fruit" was interpreted as converts to Christianity. The idea being that the abiding presence of Christ would then cause a person to be a great "soul winner" or a generator of many people making professions of faith in Christ. There was no association made with this transforming our behavior to become more Christ like or loving. But it became clear to me that the fruit of Christ produced would be the moral and spiritual life of Christ which is love. This connection with the fruit produced by the VINE Jesus with the fruit of the Holy Spirit in the life of the believing Christian then made perfect sense to me. It also made clear that the Christian life totally depended on a faith relationship with Christ Jesus and not living a "will based" effort done in my own strength. Now such a life of divine LOVE, I believe does cause us to share the good news about Christ in word and deed to others in witnessing. But now witnessing becomes really an act of worship.

A spiritual experiment in seeking the Abiding of Jesus

To benefit from John 15:1-8 we need to not just have a firm grasp on what it teaches but we need to experience the presence of the Living Christ in this passage.

It is not enough that we have read the passage but that the passage has read us.   It is this that really changed my entire approach to living the Christian life day by day.

Approaching the Bible in this manner, is known as the "Sacred Reading" of scripture and its aim is not for us to know the passage but for us to experience a personal "knowing" of Jesus Christ through the passage of Scripture.

To begin this process, I want you to read out loud the passage carefully, slowly, and prayerfully.

Prayer before reading: Holy Spirit now let me hear from the Lord Jesus exactly what HE would want me to hear from the reading of this passage.   Breathe on this passage and allow it to have the power to revive and renew my faith, love, and hope.   Lord, speak to me now through this YOUR WORD. Amen

Read the passage out loud

1 "I am the true vine, and My Father is the vinedresser. 2 "Every branch in Me that does not bear fruit, He takes away; and every [branch] that bears fruit, He prunes it so that it may bear more fruit. 3 "You are already clean because of the word which I have spoken to you.

4 "Abide in Me, and I in you. As the branch cannot bear fruit of itself unless it abides in the vine, so neither [can] you unless you abide in Me.

5 "I am the vine, you are the branches; he who abides in Me and I in him, he bears much fruit, for apart from Me you can do nothing.

6 "If anyone does not abide in Me, he is thrown away as a branch and dries up; and they gather them, and cast them into the fire and they are burned.

7 "If you abide in Me, and My words abide in you, ask whatever you wish, and it will be done for you. 8 "My Father is glorified by this, that you bear much fruit, and [so] prove to be My disciples. [Jhn 15:1-8 NASB95]

Pause for one minute quietly before the Lord being sensitive to any impression or feeling that may have been stirred by the reading of the passage.

Prayer for the Second Reading - Holy Spirit now point out to me key words, thoughts, and phrases which are the most important for me to focus on now today.   Speak directly to me now through YOUR WORD.   Allow my heart to be in tune with YOUR heart for me today.   Amen

Read the passage out loud – Underline or mark any words, thoughts or phrases that stand out to you.

1 "I am the true vine, and My Father is the vinedresser. 2 "Every branch in Me that does not bear fruit, He takes away; and every [branch] that bears fruit, He prunes it so that it may bear more fruit. 3 "You are already clean because of the word which I have spoken to you.

4 "Abide in Me, and I in you. As the branch cannot bear fruit of itself unless it abides in the vine, so neither [can] you unless you abide in Me.

5 "I am the vine, you are the branches; he who abides in Me and I in him, he bears much fruit, for apart from Me you can do nothing.

6 "If anyone does not abide in Me, he is thrown away as a branch and dries up; and they gather them, and cast them into the fire and they are burned.

7 "If you abide in Me, and My words abide in you, ask whatever you wish, and it will be done for you. 8 "My Father is glorified by this, that you bear much fruit, and [so] prove to be My disciples. [Jhn 15:1-8 NASB95]

Pause for one minute and see if you have any impressions or leadings based on this reading of Scripture. If so, make note of them here.

Why do you think these particular words, thoughts, or phrases were highlighted by the Holy Spirit during this reading of the Scripture?

Prayer for the Third Reading - LORD, YOUR child is listening and desires to hear YOU speak to me through YOUR WORD this day. Holy Spirit, help me hear the WORD as personal and pointed towards me in my life and circumstances. Amen

Read the passage out loud and put your name into the passage to personalize it.

1 "(Your Name ____________)I am your true vine, and My Father is your vinedresser. 2 " (Your Name ____________) Every branch in Me that does not bear fruit, your Father takes away; and every [branch] that bears fruit, your Father in heaven prunes it so that you may bear more fruit. 3 " (Your Name ____________) You are already clean because of the word which I have spoken to you.

4 ""(Your Name ____________) Abide in Me, and I in you. As the branch cannot bear fruit of itself unless it abides in the vine, so neither [can] you "(Your Name ____________) unless you abide in Me.

5 ""(Your Name ____________) I am the vine, you are the branches; if you "(Your Name ____________) abides in Me and I in you, "(Your Name ____________) will bear much fruit, for apart from Me you "(Your Name ____________) you can do nothing.

6 "If you "(Your Name ____________) do not abide in Me, you "(Your Name ____________) will be thrown away as a branch and dries up; and they gather them, and cast them into the fire and they are burned.

7 "If you "(Your Name ____________) abide in Me, and My words abide in you, ask whatever you "(Your Name ____________) wish, and it will be done for you. 8 "My Father is glorified by this, that if you "(Your Name ____________) bear much fruit, and [so] prove to be My disciple. [Jhn 15:1-8 NASB95]

Pause for one minute quietly before the Lord being sensitive to any impression or feeling that may have been stirred by the reading of the passage.

Fourth Reading of the Scripture

Prayer for the fourth reading: Lord Jesus Christ, let me not be just one who hears YOUR WORD but one that acts on it in true faith. Show me exactly the most important application of this passage of Scripture to my life at the current time. Amen

Read the passage out loud

1 "I am the true vine, and My Father is the vinedresser. 2 "Every branch in Me that does not bear fruit, He takes away; and every [branch] that bears fruit, He prunes it so that it may bear more fruit. 3 "You are already clean because of the word which I have spoken to you.

4 "Abide in Me, and I in you. As the branch cannot bear fruit of itself unless it abides in the vine, so neither [can] you unless you abide in Me.

5 "I am the vine, you are the branches; he who abides in Me and I in him, he bears much fruit, for apart from Me you can do nothing.

6 "If anyone does not abide in Me, he is thrown away as a branch and dries up; and they gather them, and cast them into the fire and they are burned.

7 "If you abide in Me, and My words abide in you, ask whatever you wish, and it will be done for you. 8 "My Father is glorified by this, that you bear much fruit, and [so] prove to be My disciples. [Jhn 15:1-8 NASB95]

Pause for one minute quietly before the Lord being sensitive to any impression or feeling that may have been stirred by the reading of the passage.

What change you think the Lord is asking YOU to make in your thoughts, words, attitudes, or actions?

Final Reading of the Scripture

Prayer: Lord let me quick to listen to YOUR WORD and allow this WORD to change me moment by moment.   Amen

Read the passage out loud

1 "I am the true vine, and My Father is the vinedresser. 2 "Every branch in Me that does not bear fruit, He takes away; and every [branch] that bears fruit, He prunes it so that it may bear more fruit. 3 "You are already clean because of the word which I have spoken to you.

4 "Abide in Me, and I in you. As the branch cannot bear fruit of itself unless it abides in the vine, so neither [can] you unless you abide in Me.

5 "I am the vine, you are the branches; he who abides in Me and I in him, he bears much fruit, for apart from Me you can do nothing.

6 "If anyone does not abide in Me, he is thrown away as a branch and dries up; and they gather them, and cast them into the fire and they are burned.

7 "If you abide in Me, and My words abide in you, ask whatever you wish, and it will be done for you. 8 "My Father is glorified by this, that you bear much fruit, and [so] prove to be My disciples. [Jhn 15:1-8 NASB95]

Pause for one minute quietly before the Lord being sensitive to any impression or feeling that may have been stirred by the reading of the passage. Just rest before the Lord and be at HiS feet.

Thank the Lord for speaking to you in HIS Word,

Another part of Sacred Reading of the Scriptures is to pray the scriptures back to God.   Here is an example of a prayer based on John 15:1-8.

1 "I am the true vine, and My Father is the vinedresser. 2 "Every branch in Me that does not bear fruit, He takes away; and every [branch] that bears fruit, He prunes it so that it may bear more fruit. 3 "You are already clean because of the word which I have spoken to you. 4 "Abide in Me, and I in you. As the branch cannot bear fruit of itself unless it abides in the vine, so neither [can] you unless you abide in Me. 5 "I am the vine, you are the branches; he who abides in Me and I in him, he bears much fruit, for apart from Me you can do nothing. 6 "If anyone does not abide in Me, he is thrown away as a branch and dries up; and they gather them, and cast them into the fire and they are burned. 7 "If you abide in Me, and My words abide in you, ask whatever you wish, and it will be done for you. 8 "My Father is glorified by this, that you bear much fruit, and [so] prove to be My disciples. [Jhn 15:1-8 NASB95]

Prayer based on John 15:1-8

LORD Jesus thank you for being the VINE and connecting me to YOU so that YOUR LIFE can flow into me and overflow out of me.   It is hard to believe LORD Jesus that YOU would allow such an intimate relationship to exist in my life. Thank YOU for YOUR grace that allows for such a union and communion of our lives.

Good Father in heaven, thank YOU for being the faithful and good Vinedresser, caring for my growth and enabling me to bear more of the fruit of LOVE in my life. YOU keep me from being trodden into the mud, lacking sunshine, and lifting me up out of my troubles into the light of YOUR loving care and direction.   YOU focus the life of the LORD Jesus in me and maximize my ability to be effective in my faith.   Thank YOU, Father, for YOUR care of me!

LORD Jesus, thank YOU for YOUR cleansing WORD of forgiveness, grace, mercy, and love. Lord Jesus show me how to abide in YOU and make me aware of how YOU are already abiding in me. My life is YOUR life and YOUR life is my life, intimately intertwined so that YOUR LIFE in me can bear fruit through me!   LORD, make me aware that apart from YOU I can accomplish nothing at all. LORD, outside of YOU there is nothing but death and destruction.   Keep me from ever having any thoughts of leaving YOU.   YOU alone are my hope and life.

LORD, show me how to have YOUR words so deeply in me and guiding my prayers that they become "Kingdom focused" and powerful in bringing YOUR will from heaven to earth. Teach me to have "abiding prayers".

LORD, allow my life to be filled with the experience and expression of YOUR life and love so that the true nature, awesome character, and attributes of the Heavenly Father will be magnified in me. Amen

Write your own prayer based on John 15:1-8

The purpose of this book is for people to not just gain "ideas" but to experience the living presence of the Lord Jesus and for HIS fruit to overflow out of us.

The practice of the Sacred Reading of scripture is one of the practices that have helped people "abide" and bear "fruit" and therefore it seemed a good idea to introduce the practice here as we meditation on this key passage together.   I hope you will give it a try.

Journal on Chapter Three[5] - Day Three

1. Was this exercise in "Sacred Reading" helpful? How or why?

2. Did you experience the presence of the Living Christ by this process of meditating on the scriptures?   Describe your experience both positive and negative.

3. If you were to do this exercise differently, how would you do it to be more effective for you?

Personal Journal – Day 3

This chapter provided the key experiences of the Living reality of Christ in me that transformed my Christian life from attempting to serve Christ in my own strength to actually in faith seeking to experience of the LORD being in me and wanting to overflow HIS love and life out of me. The Holy Spirit used the sacred reading of scripture and praying the scriptures back to the LORD that brought to me a greater revelation of Christ living in me and through me. These practices are a significant part of my walk with the Lord today.

Chapter Four: Who is Jesus and who is the Father? – Day Four

---

[5] Resources on Sacred Reading – **A Journal of Sacred Readings: Spiritual Formation through Personal Encounters with Scripture** by Kenneth Boa; Prayer Tools – **How To Do the Lectio Divina** - https://downloads.24-7prayer.com/prayer_course/2019/resources/pdfs/21%20How%20to%20do%20the%20Lectio%20Divina.pdf

The first truth is that we must know is who is Jesus and the role of God the Father in giving us an effective and meaningful life. Without knowing who Jesus is, we cannot be effective in abiding.

Without understanding the Heavenly Father's key role, we will not fully comprehend the process of "abiding".

""I am the true vine, and My Father is the vinedresser." John 15:1[6]

Jesus is the true vine and God the Father is the vinedresser or gardener.

Since Jesus says that HE is the "true" vine there must be at least one "false vine".

The inspiration of the use of the vine may have been because there was a golden vine on the Temple door. This proclaimed that the temple and the leaders of Israel were the "true vine" through which the life of God could be experienced.

"This feature was one of the most remarkable in all the Temple precincts. Middot records that "A golden vine stood over the entrance to the sanctuary, trained over posts; and whosoever gave a leaf, or a berry, or a cluster as a freewill-offering, he brought it and the priests hung it thereon."

Christ may have alluded to this very feature of the Temple when he said in John 15. 1: "I am the true vine."[7]

Christ Jesus may be thinking of Jeremiah 2:21 in which Israel instead of being the faithful planted vine of the LORD, has become a foreign vine bearing ungodly fruit. Clearly, this was the case of the state of Israel in the days of Jesus Christ because of the rejection of the leadership of HIM as the Messiah or Christ.

Christ Jesus is claiming here that HE is the true Israel, the faithful vine, and the one that will now be the source of a great harvest from God. The LORD Jesus will be the source of life, fruitfulness, nourishment, and strength.   Judaism in HIS day had cut themselves off from HIM who was the true vine and therefore could not produce any "kingdom fruit" for the glory of the Father in Heaven. [8]

It is clear that Psalm 80 may also have been on Christ Jesus' mind in seeing Himself as the "true vine"

---

[6] (3) The expression I am the bread of life (6:35)is the first of seven similar claims, each with egō eimi ('I am') and a predicate. The other six (plus minor variations) are: I am the light of the world (8:12), the gate (10:7, 9), the good shepherd (10:11, 14), the resurrection and the life (11:25), the way and the truth and the life (14:6), the true vine (15:1, 5)[6] The Gospel According To John by D.A. Carson
[7] https://www.ritmeyer.com/product/image-library/buildings/temples/golden-vine-of-herods-temple/
https://www.biblestudytools.com/commentaries/gills-exposition-of-the-bible/john-15-1.html

[8] In the Old Testament the vine is a common symbol for Israel, the covenant people of God (Ps. 80:9–16; Is. 5:1–7; 27:2ff.; Je. 2:21; 12:10ff.; Ezk. 15:1–8; 17:1–21; 19:10–14; Ho. 10:1–2). Most remarkable is the fact that whenever historic Israel is referred to under this figure it is the vine's failure to produce good fruit that is emphasized, along with the corresponding threat of God's judgment on the nation. Now, in contrast to such failure, Jesus claims, 'I am the true vine', i.e. the one to whom Israel pointed, the one that brings forth good fruit. Jesus has already, in principle, superseded the temple, the Jewish feasts, Moses, various holy sites; here he supersedes Israel as the very locus of the people of God. (A similar contrast between Israel and Jesus is developed in various ways in the Synoptics: e.g. in the temptation narrative, Mt. 4:1–11 par.)[8] The Gospel According To John by D.A. Carson

Restore us, O God Almighty;
make your face shine upon us,
that we may be saved.
You brought a vine out of Egypt;
you drove out the nations and planted it …
Return to us, O God Almighty!
Look down from heaven and see!
Watch over this vine,
the root your right hand has planted,
the son [the Heb. word may mean 'stock' or 'branch'] you have raised up for yourself.
Your vine is cut down, it is burned with fire;
at your rebuke your people perish.
Let your hand rest on the man at your right hand,
the son of man you have raised up for yourself.

(Ps. 80:7–8, 14–17)

Here we see the image of the "VINE" and the "son of man" who becomes the Savior.

If I am looking to anyone outside Jesus to be the source of life, fruitfulness, nourishment, and strength I am connected to a "false vine" which will never produce the good fruit of true loving holiness in my life.

This is the key question for my life!

<u>Outside of Christ Jesus where do I turn to find energy, effectiveness, and enjoyment?</u>

<u>What do I believe will give me success outside of my faith relationship with Jesus Christ?</u>

This is my idol. We all have idols.

Tim Keller identifies four ways we can find idols in our lives.

1. What do we imagine doing that captures our attention and focus? What do we daydream about doing?

2. How do we spend our money?   Are our finances focused on the kingdom of God or something else?

3. How do you handle it when God says "No" to your prayers?   Did you want something more than God's will? Was God just a" means" to get what you ultimately valued.

4. Look at your most uncomfortable emotions. Do they reflect desiring or valuing something more than you should?[9]

John Piper defines an idol as: "Well, I'll try. Let's start with a definition. I think to cover all the cases, we should probably define an idol (and I think this is a biblical definition) as anything that we come to rely on for some blessing, or help, or guidance in the place of a wholehearted reliance on the true and living God."[10]

Reflect for a moment. Are there things in your life that you depend on to gain success more than your relationship with the "VINE" Jesus?

If so, this may be an idol in your life.

It should be Jesus only Jesus that I depend on as my Savior, hope, helper, healer, leader, teacher, prophet, priest, and king.   I will not do this perfectly, but it is the goal I should strive to see more and more manifested in my life.

The more I come to know and experience Jesus as the source of healthy and holy life in me the more my life overflows with the divine LOVE.

The Apostle Paul seems to reflect this when he says:

""I have been crucified with Christ Jesus; and it is no longer I who live, but Christ Jesus lives in me; and the life which I now live in the flesh I live by faith in the Son of God, who loved me and gave Himself up for me." Galatians 2:20

Galatians 2:20 the LORD gave me at a time of spiritual crisis where I felt that all was lost and I had no hope left, yet in the middle of the greatest crisis of faith in my life, the Holy Spirit gave this verse to me and renewed my faith and sanity.   At that moment I became aware of Christ living in me.

---

[9] http://lhim.org/blog/2012/10/02/tim-keller-identifying-idols/

[10] https://www.desiringgod.org/interviews/what-is-an-idol

Paul expands on this in Philippians when he says "4 although I myself [could boast as] having confidence even in the flesh. If anyone else thinks he is confident in the flesh, I [have] more [reason:] ... 7 But whatever things were gain to me, these things I have counted as loss because of Christ. 8 More than that, I count all things to be loss in view of the surpassing value of knowing Christ Jesus my Lord, for whom I have suffered the loss of all things, and count them [mere] rubbish, so that I may gain Christ, 9 and may be found in Him, not having a righteousness of my own derived from [the] Law, but that which is through faith in Christ, the righteousness which [comes] from God on the basis of faith, 10 that I may know Him and the power of His resurrection and the fellowship of His sufferings, being conformed to His death;" [Phl 3:4, 7-10 NASB20]

Only when we grow in our vision of Jesus can we grow in our abiding in HIM. It is not "will power" that fuels the Christian life but our experience of "seeing Jesus" more clearly. The better my vision, the greater my love for the Lord Jesus, and then following HIM happens automatically.

There was a sermon called "That's My King" that always has helped me remember the greatness of the Lord Christ Jesus by Dr. Lockridge.

Read this out loud carefully and prayerfully asking the Lord to deepen your vision of the greatness of Christ Jesus.

Circle any description of the Lord Jesus that emotionally moves you,

Write out why you think this vision of Jesus is important to you.

"That's My King". -A message by Rev. Dr. Shadrach Meshach Lockridge (1913 – 2000).

"My King was born King.

The Bible says my King is a seven-way King:

He's the King of the Jews.

That's a racial King.

He's the King of Israel.

That's a national King.

He's the King of righteousness.

He's the King of the ages.

He's the King of Heaven.

He's the King of Glory.

He's the King of Kings and

He is the Lord of Lords.

Now, that's my King.

Well, I wonder, do you know Him?

Do you know Him?

Don't try to mislead me, do you know

my King?

David said, "The heavens declare the

glory of God and the firmament

showeth His handiwork."

My King is the only one whom...

There's no means of measure can

define His limitless love.

No farseeing telescope can bring

into visibility the coastline of His

shoreless supplies.

No barrier can hinder Him from

pouring out His blessings.

Well, Well, He's enduringly strong.

He's entirely sincere.

He's eternally steadfast.

He's immortally graceful.

He's imperially powerful.

He's impartially merciful.

That's my King

He's God's Son.

He's the sinner's Savior.

He's the centerpiece of civilization.

He stands alone in Himself.

He's august and He's unique.

He's unparalleled.

He's unprecedented.

He's supreme.

He's pre-eminent.

He's the loftiest idea in literature.

He's the highest personality in
philosophy.

He's the supreme problem in
higher criticism.

He's the fundamental doctrine of
true theology.

He's the core and necessity of
spiritual religion.

That's my King!

He's the miracle of the age.

He's the superlative of everything

good that you choose to call Him.

Well, He's the only one able to supply

all of our needs simultaneously.

He supplies strength to the weak.

He's available for the tempted and

the tried.

He sympathizes and He saves.

He is our guard and guide.

He heals the sick.

He cleanses the lepers.

He forgives sinners.

He discharges debtors.

He delivers the captives.

He defends the feeble.

He blesses the young.

He serves the unfortunate.

He regards the aged.

He rewards the diligent and

He beautifies the meek.

Do you know Him?

Well! My King is the Key of

knowledge.

He's the Wellspring of wisdom.

He's the Doorway of deliverance.

He's the Pathway of peace.

He's the Roadway of righteousness.

He's the Highway of holiness.

He's the Gateway of glory.

He's the Master of the mighty.

He's the Captain of the conquerors.

He's the Head of the heroes.

He's the Leader of the legislators.

He's the Overseer of the

overcomers.

He's the Governor of governors.

He's the Prince of princes.

He's the King of kings and

He's the Lord of lords.

That's my King! Yeah! Yeah!

That's my King. My King.

Yeah, His office is manifold.

His promise is sure.

His life is matchless.

His goodness is limitless.

His mercy is everlasting.

His love never changes.

His word is enough.

His grace is sufficient.

His reign is righteous.

And His yoke is easy and His

burden is light.

Well… I wish I could describe Him

to you!

But He, He's indescribable. He's

indescribable, Yes!

He, He's incomprehensible.

He's invincible.

He's irresistible!

I've come to tell you, the heaven of

heavens cannot contain Him let

alone a man explain Him.

You can't get Him out of your mind.

You can't get Him off of your hand.

You can't out live Him and

You can't live without Him.

Well, the Pharisees couldn't stand

Him, but they found out they

couldn't stop Him.

Pilate couldn't find any fault in Him.

The witnesses couldn't get their testimonies to agree.

Herod couldn't kill Him.

Death couldn't handle Him and the

grave couldn't hold Him.

That's my King, yeah!

He always has been, and he

always will be.

I'm talking about… He has no

predecessor, and He'll have no

successor.

There was nobody before Him and

there'll be nobody after Him.

You can't impeach Him, and He's

not going to resign.

That's my King!

Great is the Lord! That's my king!

Thine, thine is the Kingdom and

the power and the glory. Yeah!

Thine is the Kingdom and the

power and the glory.

For ever and ever and ever and

ever.

How long is that?

And ever and ever, and ever and

ever.

And when you get through with all

of the forevers, then Amen!"

If that's how Dr Lockridge

described the Lord Jesus while seeing Him

'through a glass, darkly' here on

Earth, how do you think he'd

describe the Lord Jesus now he's seen Him

face to face in Heaven?[11]

Journal notes on this message.   What strikes you most about Christ Jesus from this message?

This is the VINE that we as branches are connected to and get our life from. Do you know HIM?

This is the Lord King Jesus who we have a connection with and are in relationship with. Wow!

---

[11] http://emmanuel-eastleigh.org/wp-content/uploads/2009/06/thats-my-king-video-transcript.pdf

You can listen to this message online at and if you can do so now!
https://www.youtube.com/watch?v=yzqTFNfeDnE&feature=emb_logo

The greater our vision of the Lord Jesus the less anything will tempt us as an idol. The last chapter in this book is designed to help you grow in a fuller and greater vision of the Lord Jesus. You may want to turn to it now if you would like to grow in a more dynamic vision of the greatness, goodness, and grace of the Lord Jesus.

Ask the Holy Spirit to increase YOUR wonder and awe of who the Lord Jesus is to you in your personal life.

We are not saved by a doctrine or teaching, although we have to accept the key doctrinal truths about the Lord Jesus to be a Christian.

But one can accept a doctrine and not know the person. To have life in us we must be connected to the living person of the Christ Jesus who died for our sins and was raised from the dead. We must turn to HIM as our living High Priest in heaven for help and guidance in times of need, trusting in HIS compassion and care for us. We need to see that HE is the source of all our life, love, and power.

All who call out to the Lord Jesus Christ believing that HE died for their sins and was raised from the dead and now want HIM to be in their life as the ultimate source of truth, the ultimate forgiver of their sins, and the ultimate leader of their life, who ask HIM to come an dwell in them, be their life; will be connected and will have the eternal life of God the Son who became the Son of God; Jesus in them.

Have you with sincerity and faith cried out to the LORD Jesus to save YOU? If not, now is a good time to do that and get connected to the Vine and have HIS life invade YOU. If you have, then it is good to remind yourself of this faith and return to YOUR "first love".

28 "Come to Me, all who are weary and heavy-laden, and I will give you rest. 29 "Take My yoke upon you and learn from Me, for I am gentle and humble in heart, and YOU WILL FIND REST FOR YOUR SOULS. 30 "For My yoke is easy and My burden is light." [Mat 11:28-30 NASB95]

The second truth of this first verse is that God the Father is the "vinedresser" or gardener. The heavenly Father takes care of the vineyard and HE oversees, cares for, nurtures, trims, and defends the garden and the vine (Matthew 21:33).

The eternal loving Father has planted HIS SON, giving HIM to be the source of life, grace, mercy, and love to HIS people.   The effective Divine Gardener has great investment, care, and love for HIS vineyard. HE manages the vineyard to produce the greatest amount of production and profit for HIS kingdom.

The wise and compassionate Father is the ultimately good, great, committed, caring, and involved gardener of my life in Christ Jesus.

How is God the Father active as a gardener in your life?

Is relating to God as your heavenly Father difficult because of the failures of your earthly father?

How can you more fully accept the ideal Father in heaven and trust that HE is always working for YOUR good?

Firmly believing in the God as YOUR good Father is a vital part of living a life of faith in Christ Jesus. The theology of Jesus Christ is centered on the idea of God being a good, gracious, great, and loving heavenly Father.

In a sermon by Randy Hyde, Pastor, Pulaski Heights Baptist Church, in Little Rock he summarized how our vision of God as our good heavenly Father is critical to our living a life of faith.

"Our heavenly Father, through the atoning life and death of his only unique Son, stands ready to bless us, to reach down and touch us in a way that no other can do.

Think about it… the God who created the world and cast the stars into space, the God whose majesty is seen in the highest mountains and whose mystery is revealed in the deepest oceans, "the God who blessed the world with language and then confounded it with many tongues,"3 is the same God who blesses you and me… the same God you and I, because of the testimony and life of Jesus, can call Our Father.

As a child reaches out its hand in trust to a loving father guiding its first steps, we can reach out our hand to God. For God is Our Father, and he calls to us in love. I encourage you to place your hand in the hand of God. It will not be without scars, but with it HE will tenderly accept and bless you.

O Lord our God, our Father, may we trust your tender care… through Christ our Lord, Amen."[12]

Prayer

Living Triune great, good, and eternal Redeeming Creator, give me practical and real faith in the LORD Jesus to be the one and only source in my life that can produce in me wisdom,

---

[12] https://goodfaithmedia.org/what-jesus-said-about-the-fatherhood-of-god-cms-21844/

righteousness, love, holiness, purpose, and redemption. Help my heart to see that Christ has a monopoly on everything good and that the only thing that I have to boast about is that HE is in me and I am in HIM (1 Corinthians 1:30-31).

Good gardening Eternal Father, King of the Universe, help me believe that regardless of how chaotic my life appears, YOU are watching over, caring, and providing me daily opportunities to grow and give in a useful way. YOU are working all things out for good. Help me trust YOU heavenly Father when I am in the dark that YOU never sleep or slumber but are a faithful Watchman over my daily life and soul every moment of every day.

Give me faith LORD Jesus to trust YOU to be my vine and the Father to be my vinedresser.   Amen

Spiritual Exercises

9 "So I say to you, ask, and it will be given to you; seek, and you will find; knock, and it will be opened to you. 10 "For everyone who asks, receives; and he who seeks, finds; and to him who

knocks, it will be opened. 11 "Now suppose one of you fathers is asked by his son for a fish; he will not give him a snake instead of a fish, will he? 12 "Or [if] he is asked for an egg, he will not give him a scorpion, will he? 13 "If you then, being evil, know how to give good gifts to your children, how much more will [your] heavenly Father give the Holy Spirit to those who ask Him?" [Luke 11:9-13 NASB95]

11 And He said, "A man had two sons. 12 "The younger of them said to his father, 'Father, give me the share of the estate that falls to me.' So he divided his wealth between them. 13 "And not many days later, the younger son gathered everything together and went on a journey into a distant country, and there he squandered his estate with loose living. 14 "Now when he had spent everything, a severe famine occurred in that country, and he began to be impoverished. 15 "So he went and hired himself out to one of the citizens of that country, and he sent him into his fields to feed swine. 16 "And he would have gladly filled his stomach with the pods that the swine were eating, and no one was giving [anything] to him. 17 "But when he came to his senses, he said, 'How many of my father's hired men have more than enough bread, but I am dying here with hunger! 18 'I will get up and go to my father, and will say to him, "Father, I have sinned against heaven, and in your sight; 19 I am no longer worthy to be called your son; make me as one of your hired men."' 20 "So he got up and came to his father. But while he was still a long way off, his father saw him and felt compassion [for him,] and ran and embraced him and kissed him. 21 "And the son said to him, 'Father, I have sinned against heaven and in your sight; I am no longer worthy to be called your son.' 22 "But the father said to his slaves, 'Quickly bring out the best robe and put it on him, and put a ring on his hand and sandals on his feet; 23 and bring the fattened calf, kill it, and let us eat and celebrate; 24 for this son of mine was dead and has come to life again; he was lost and has been found.' And they began to celebrate. 25 "Now his older son was in the field, and when he came and approached the house, he heard music and dancing. 26 "And he summoned one of the servants and [began] inquiring what these things could be. 27 "And he said to him, 'Your brother has come, and your father has killed the fattened calf because he has received him back safe and sound.' 28 "But he became angry and was not willing to go in; and his father came out and [began] pleading with him. 29 "But he answered and said to his father, 'Look! For so many years I have been serving you and I have never neglected a command of yours; and [yet] you have never given me a young goat, so that I might celebrate with my friends; 30 but when this son of yours came, who has devoured your wealth with prostitutes, you killed the fattened calf for him.' 31 "And he said to him, 'Son, you have always been with me, and all that is mine is yours. 32 'But we had to celebrate and rejoice, for this brother of yours was dead and [has begun] to live, and [was] lost and has been found.'" [Luk 15:11-32 NASB95]

Do a "Sacred Reading" on these passages of Scripture and seek the Holy Spirit to open YOU to see God the Father working on your behalf and caring about you more than you ever thought was possible.

Review of how to do a "Sacred Reading"

1. Pause before each reading of the scripture and seek an awareness of Jesus' presence in you.

2. Pray for the Holy Spirit to speak to you when you read the passage. Always pause and pray before each of the reading of the scripture.

3. Read the Scriptures out loud carefully and prayerfully

     A. First Reading of The Scriptures seek to paraphrase the passage into your own words

     B. Second Reading of Scripture mark any words or phrases that stand out and seek to understand what God is attempting to tell you in those words and phrases.

     C. Third Reading of Scripture put your name into the passage, so it is God personally speaking it to you.

     D. Fourth Reading of Scripture seek for one concrete application of the passage into your life.

     E. Fifth Reading of the Scripture use it to frame a prayer to God using the passage as the framework for what you ask for in your prayers.

4. Pray for the Lord to reveal HIMSELF personally to YOU in the scripture. Ask to hear HIS voice.

5. Pause to just be still and know HE is with you.   Record any impressions or thoughts that come to you during this time.   End in singing a song of praise.

Go through this process with Luke 11:9-13 and Luke 15:11-32 with a focus on growing in a vision of God as YOUR good, great, and gracious heavenly Father.

Questions – Day Four

1. What outside of Jesus do you trust in to give to you, life, productiveness, and effectiveness?

2. Do you trust that God the Father is a good gardener in your life? Do you believe HE cares for you?   Why or why not?

Personal Journal for Chapter Four

I have always found it easier to relate to the Lord Jesus than to God the Father. My dad struggled with alcohol and a temper. Eventually after decades and about ten years before his death he got connected to Jesus and became a fruitful branch in the vine, demonstrating substantial love to everyone.   By the grace of the Lord, we were reconciled before he died.   But the last vision of God that I thought I could ever relate to was as a Father because all of my memories of my dad were stained with a lot of abuse.   But the Holy Spirit has been helping me more and more to not only see that greatness of Jesus but to trust in the heavenly Father to be one who can be trusted to want to provide good things for my life.   More so today than at any time I have come to see God as a good, great, and gracious spiritual "Daddy" which I would have thought impossible. I know that it has to be the Lord in me making that change because humanly it would be outside of any change I could ever make or want to make.   Thank YOU, FATHER, in heaven for being patient with me and helping see YOU as trustworthy and loving me.   Please help this to continue since it is such a vital reality for me to accept.   Amen

Chapter Five – The Heavenly Father's Work in our relationship with Christ – Day 5

""Every branch in Me that does not bear fruit, He takes away; and every branch that bears fruit, He prunes it so that it may bear more fruit." John 15:2`

The person who is a branch of the VINE Jesus is one who has professed that HE is the Christ, God the Son and who has become the Son of God. (John 1:1-18). <u>Every true believer abides in the VINE</u> of Jesus and the life of Jesus abides in everyone who is in a trusting relationship with HIM.

I am a branch if I have claimed Christ Jesus as my DIVINE personal Prophet, Priest, and King. By faith I am united with HIM in a spiritual and real connection.

This objective reality is one that at times I may recognize in my experience and at other times may seem only a distant theological concept. But the reality of that relationship does not change based on my subjective awareness of it, movement by moment. The VINE will be producing fruit through my life before I am even aware of John 15:1-8, have read it, or comprehend in anyway its meaning. The reality of the relationship does not depend on my doctrinal knowledge or understanding.

I can see the life of the Lord producing fruit in me since I came to accept him when I was seven. I did not recognize it then as the life of Christ manifesting itself through me but now, I can look back and see the attitudes, actions, and words of LOVE that occurred was not "me" but "HIM in me".

The LORD will always bear fruit in every person who has a true relationship with HIM. This occurs even when that person is unaware that what is being produced in them has its source in the life of the risen LORD in them. Once we understand this truth, we can get a whole new understanding of our spiritual lives.

If I have a true faith, trust, commitment, and acceptance of the Lord Jesus as my one source of hope, forgiveness, and life to some degree, then to that degree, the overflow of Christ's love and life overflows out of me. Every person who really believes in the Christ Jesus will bear some fruit of the Spirit in their lives. The LORD never fails to bear fruit in a true believer.

The big question is "Do I know HIM"! Not just a doctrine about HIM; but do I know HIM. If I know HIM then I am a branch connected to HIM and this will bear some fruit in my life.

Now some who claim to have such a relationship do not bear the fruit of Christ Jesus. This fruit is love (1 Corinthians 13; Gal 5:22). It is possible to have the right doctrine about Christ Jesus but not personally know HIM in a living relationship. Such a "faith" cannot save anyone and is without the fruit of love (James 2). There are many who "profess" faith in Christ but are not possessed by Jesus Christ in a real relationship.

To the degree that people have God's unconditional love for others and love for Jesus then to that degree we can know that they have a real relationship with Jesus. The presence of the LOVE of Christ in us for HIM and others is the best evidence that we have a real relationship with the Living Christ. This love will not be perfect, sometimes stronger, and sometimes weaker; but while imperfect it is real.

22 If anyone does not love the Lord, he is to be accursed. Maranatha! [1Co 16:22 NASB20]

8 The one who does not love does not know God, because God is love. ... 20 If someone says, "I love God," and [yet] he hates his brother [or sister,] he is a liar; for the one who does not love his brother [and sister] whom he has seen, cannot love God, whom he has not seen.

[1Jo 4:8, 20 NASB20]

When people have no fruit of love in their lives then their professed faith is not real faith (James 2).

Most every translation of John 15:2 translates the Greek word (airo) as "He takes away".   This would seem to be an understandable translation in light of John 15:6 in which it is clear that some branches that do not abide and therefore are without the fruit of love face a judgment of fire.

The branch without fruit would be a person who made an outward profession of faith in the LORD Jesus but never truly was possessed by the LORD Jesus. Such would be the case of Judas and others who leave the faith after professing it. (Matthew 13:21). Their apostasy from the faith showed they never really had the faith or a true personal relationship with Christ Jesus.

Yet the word translated "cut off" has a primary meaning of to "lift up" or "carry".   Because of this, it is not the only possible translation of this verse.   Christ's words could be translated:

""Every branch in Me that does not bear fruit, *He lifts up*, and every branch that bears fruit, He prunes it so that it may bear more fruit." John 15:2

<u>If this is what it means this verse would mean that the Infinite Father would be lifting this branch up out of the darkness where it cannot bear fruit to a place where it would bear fruit.</u>

This would be a translation that focuses on the idea of the branch being "in the Vine" as more than a formal outward profession but a real spiritual connection. This would seem to fit better Jesus' teaching in the gospel of John that states clearly, HE does not lose any of those who are truly HIS disciples.

27 "My sheep listen to My voice, and I know them, and they follow Me; 28 and I give them eternal life, and they will never perish; and no one will snatch them out of My hand. 29 "My Father, who has given [them] to Me, is greater than all; and no one is able to snatch [them] out of the Father's hand. [Jhn 10:27-29 NASB20]

In this case the lack of fruit of the branch would be temporary and the lifting up would allow it to bear the fruit of Christ's love.

That the great GARDENER of our souls does do this is without question.   For when a branch does bear some fruit, then HE "prunes" that branch to make it more productive. The word for prunes is καθαίρει (<u>kathairei</u>) which means really that the Great loving Divine Father cleans us. [13]

This may well be the chastising discipline promised to all God's children for their good and the <u>increase of their productivity as</u> disciples given to us by the author of Hebrews.

[13] http://greekbible.com/index.php
https://biblehub.com/commentaries/john/15-2.htm

"You have not yet resisted to the point of shedding blood in your striving against sin; and you have forgotten the exhortation which is addressed to you as sons, "MY SON, DO NOT REGARD LIGHTLY THE DISCIPLINE OF THE LORD, NOR FAINT WHEN YOU ARE REPROVED BY HIM; <u>FOR THOSE WHOM THE LORD LOVES HE DISCIPLINES</u>, AND HE SCOURGES EVERY SON WHOM HE RECEIVES." It is for discipline that you endure; God deals with you as with sons; for what son is there whom his father does not discipline? But if you are without discipline, of which all have become partakers, then you are illegitimate children and not sons. (Hebrews 12:4-6)

I can only bear fruit because I am "in the VINE" who is Jesus" because the power of life and love are in my union and communion with HIM.   That connection is vital for me becoming a person of unconditional love for other people and passionate love for the one true TRIUNE God.   If I am without love in me then this may indicate that I am not really in a life-giving relationship "IN the VINE".

Perhaps, I am only professing faith in the LORD Jesus without really being possessed by the LORD Jesus. This is possible and I need to be radically honest with the state of my soul and the presence of love in my life.   When I lack love for God and other people, I need to examine myself to see if I really am in a real relationship by faith with the LORD Jesus (2 Corinthians 13:5).

Sadly, some people who are self-justifying and manifest little love would never consider that they are not in the VINE, while others have such sensitive consciences that even though other see them as massively loving, they doubt the validity of their faith.   It seems as those who most need to take heed of the warning are most likely to ignore it and those that should rejoice in how Christ is manifesting HIS love in them, more seldom to become plagued by doubts.

I had a dear friend who today is dancing with Jesus having passed away over a decade now. He was a man who showed great love to many people, generous, caring, and kind.   I really saw the love of Christ in him, but he always was concerned about the legitimate nature of his faith. He totally trusts the payment of Christ for his sins, had a good doctrinal understanding of grace, and was a student of the Bible.   However, as he examined himself, he always doubted himself and feared being lost in the end. I always told him he was going to be one of the most surprised saints in heaven when he was greeted by the Lord with a loud "Good and faithful servant, enter into the joy of the Lord.

Some people that never doubt their being in the VINE need to do some deeper reflection and some who are always afraid they are not in the VINE normally need to be encouraged and really take note of how the LORD is using them.

None of us loves perfectly or are experiencing the abiding perfectly because none of us believe or love perfectly yet. The Father cleanses us to make us more able to be vessels of deeper faith and love.

Yet, a season of lacking fruit, what is called a "dark night of the soul" may occur in a true believer's life and the loving and compassionate Heavenly Father will lift me up and carry me into the light where I can experience and share Jesus' love with others again.

I went into a "dark night of the soul" for the first time in my second year of Bible College.   I feared I would become an atheist. Yet, God in HIS mercy in Christ Jesus got me through my season of doubts and anger to rest in HIM as my friend and Savior.   My faith was actually stronger after this "dark night" than before and it showed me how God uses even such difficult days as ways to grow our faith (James 1:2-4)

True Christians go through difficult spiritual crisis and struggle and then are restored by God's grace to live faith filled lives of love.

31 "Simon, Simon, behold, Satan has demanded to sift you [men] like wheat; 32 but I have prayed for you, that your faith will not fail; and you, when you have turned back, strengthen your brothers."
[Luke 22:31-32 NASB20]

The purpose of the Heavenly Gardener is to care, nurture, correct, discipline, and cleanse me so that my life may bear abundant fruit of faith filled loving actions, words, and attitudes.

God the Father has destined and determined that I will be effective in reflecting HIS love to a dark world because of the life of the LORD Jesus in me and the loving concern He has in actively being involved and watching over me.   The Father in heaven will have a productive garden!

May I become more and more aware of being connected to the LORD Jesus in a living relationship of faith and love, so that will produce in me a life worth living and rightly give HIM all the credit for every good thing that comes out of me.

May I see the intervention of the Heavenly Gardener my Father, helping me to become ever more effective in living a believing, good, noble, and praiseworthy life for HIS glory.

Father, Son, and Spirit are involved in producing in me a life reflecting the character of Jesus's love into the world (Ephesians 2:10). This is created in me by giving me a clearer and clearer revelation of the character, competence, and compassion of the One true Triune God reflected in the gospel of Jesus Christ.

Prayer

Great Living Lord Jesus, allow YOUR life to flow into me and bear fruit.

Make me more and more aware of our union and communion in the SPIRIT. Lord, I believe, help my unbelief.

Heavenly Father cleanse me so that I will bear more abundant faith, hope, and love in my life.

Help me to produce an abundant life of loving words, actions, and attitudes for YOUR glory.

Help me feel, see, and understand YOUR active work in me.

Let me hear YOUR word and believe YOUR word so that I may live in the light of YOUR word.

When I am in the dark, lift me up and allow YOUR light to shine upon me and allow me to bear fruit again.

Let me see YOU more clearly, that I may love YOU more dearly, and follow YOU more nearly in all I do.

Thank YOU for making me a branch attached to YOU. Make me fruitful. Amen

Questions – Day Five

1. Do you see the fruit of love in some way coming out of your relationship with Christ Jesus?

2. Have you ever been lifted up out of a "dark night of the soul" by the heavenly Father?

3. Have you ever seen spiritual discipline by the Heavenly Father produce greater love in your life?

Personal Journal on this chapter

My own Christian journey has been one that began with childlike faith when I was a suicidal seven year old whose physical and spiritual life was saved by a Sunday School teacher taking the time to explain John 3:16 to me, to an excited but ignorant part of the revival in the 70s called "The Jesus Movement" in which I experienced a very real encounter with the Living Christ and began sharing HIS love with others, to a doubting of my faith in my second year of Bible College in which the LORD himself delivered me from demonic lies in. a dramatic manner, and seasons of seeing the Lord in dramatic ways that I know I could never do in my own strength. The Father has lifted me out of the mud of doubt and despair more than once in this journey and been faithful in restoring me even when I had only the faith of a mustard seed. Because of this, I praise the Father in heaven for preserving my faith and allowing me to bask in the sunlight of HIS LOVE in Christ Jesus so that I may bear fruit in my life for HIS glory. Amen

""You are already clean because of the word which I have spoken to you." John 15:3

The disciples have already been cleansed by the gospel of the kingdom that has come to them in the revelation of Christ Jesus. They have been forgiven their sins, removed from the world. taken out of the false vine of the unbelieving culture and transplanted into the true vine, Jesus. They are now clean in that new relationship with HIM as the vine.

This may remind them of what HE had said earlier in the evening when HE had washed their feet.

"Jesus *said to him, "He who has bathed needs only to wash his feet, but is completely clean; and you are clean, but not all of you."" John 13:10

While the washing of feet is needed to maintain purity from the influence of the culture of unbelief the disciples have been radically removed from that culture of rebellion to now become citizens of King Jesus' kingdom.   The Lord Jesus wants them to know they can bear much fruit because they have that relationship with HIM.

"For He rescued us from the domain of darkness and transferred us to the kingdom of His beloved Son, in whom we have redemption, the forgiveness of sins." Colossians 1:13-14

Our forgiveness, purification, and spiritual cleaning comes through the power of the WORD of the gospel of the kingdom of God. The gospel of God's love for us by sending God the Son to become the Son of God, bringing us the light of HIS life, to die as the LAMB of God for our sins, and be raised from the dead to give us eternal life in joyful relationship with the Triune God, is the message that changes us forever. This divine action of pure grace has given us new birth, new life, and cleansed us of our sins.

""For God so loved the world, that He gave His only begotten Son, that whoever believes in Him shall not perish, but have eternal life." John 3:16

The basis of our abiding in the VINE Jesus, is knowing that we are in the VINE and HIS life is flowing into us. We can bear fruit because that relationship already exists by faith and grace alone. Bearing fruit is the natural result of being in the VINE.   Jesus is our life!

We must believe in Christ Jesus and keep on believing more and more in Christ Jesus. The just shall live by their faith in Christ Jesus. The greater our faith in Christ Jesus the more fruit of love we will produce in our lives.

The Father must prune from us those remaining doubts, lack of trust, idols, sins, and distractions that hinder our being as fruitful as we could be "In Christ JESUS".

But we must not forget.

We are clean in Christ Jesus!

We are forgiven in Christ Jesus!

We belong to Christ Jesus!

We are connected to Christ Jesus!

We have life in us in Christ Jesus!

Knowing that we are clean, that we are connected to the vine, that the life of the Lord Jesus flows into us, and that we are the branches of the VINE; this gives us the joyful anticipation of bearing much fruit. <u>We should be optimistic about being successful in our Christian lives because of God's faithfulness to us and the promises HE has made that HE will finish the work HE has started in us (Phil 1:6)</u>

We must grow in our faith and trust in Jesus being as our personal ultimate Prophet, High Priest, and absolute Prince of our lives. As our faith in Christ Jesus grows, we will bear more and more "kingdom fruit" in a lifestyle dominated by unconditional practical expressions of LOVE.

A book that helped me really believe that the Lord Jesus Christ had accomplished all this in my life was <u>Search For Significance</u> by Robert McGee. In this book he points out how the gospel truths can free us from the idea that our worth is based on our performance and the opinion of people rather than our worth being based on God's unchanging love in Christ Jesus. This is a vital spiritual fact.

Robert McGee points out that God's love in Christ frees us from several traps that our culture has produced that hinders us from bearing as much fruit of the gospel in our lives as we could. These false ideas and beliefs keep us from bearing the fruit of God's love found in the gospel of Jesus Christ. Here is my summary of some of the great points he makes in his book.

1. The Performance Trap – "I must meet certain standards to feel good about myself."

    This trap is overcome due to the truth that we are "justified by faith in Christ alone". God declares us righteous and puts the obedience of Christ to our account. Jesus has met all of God's standards in our place! Because we are in the "VINE" Jesus we are fully accepted and can never be condemned for our failures.

2. The Approval Trap – "I must be approved by certain others to feel good about myself."

    This false belief is overcome by the truth that we are completely reconciled and accepted by the Father based on Christ's suffering for our sins and given HIS righteousness. Our relationship in the "VINE" has been restored by God's mercy and grace alone and we did nothing to earn or deserve it. The King of the Universe has approved of me and 100% accepted me. Just as I am without one plea but that the Lord Jesus has died for me.

3. The Blame Trap – "Those who fail (including myself) are unworthy of love and deserve to be punished."

    God's answer to this problem is propitiation which means that by His death on the cross Christ satisfied God's wrath; therefore, I am deeply loved by God not because I earned it or deserved it but because "in the vine" Jesus, I have God's unconditional love (John 4:9-11)

4. The Shame Trap - Shame – "I am what I am. I cannot change. I am hopeless."

    This false belief is overcome by the truth of God's answer for shame is regeneration, which means that when we place our faith in Christ, we become a new creation. Because we have been put into the "Vine" of Jesus we will bear fruit. God in active in changing us from the inside out. Where the life of Christ exists in a person then the Lord will bring about significant change. [14]

I highly recommend that you read the book and pursue deeply studying the truths found in the book Search for Significance by Robert McGee since it was by reading this book that I really experienced at a deep emotional level the reality that God passionately loved me in Christ Jesus. [15]

[14] http://paulsohn.org/the-search-for-significance-seeing-your-true-worth-through-gods-eyes/

Prayer

Thank YOU, LORD Jesus, for making me clean. Thank YOU for forgiving me my sins! Thank YOU for giving me YOUR life in me. Help me live in this reality. Let my faith in YOU grow. Let me see YOU more clearly, love YOU more dearly, and follow YOU more dearly, that YOU may be glorified, manifested, and revealed in me. Amen

---

[15] The material on Search For Significance is now offered on-line as well. - https://www.pursuegod.org/search-for-significance/

Questions

1. Do you feel "clean" from the sins of the past or do you still struggle with a sense of shame and guilt? How do you think you could become free of these feelings of guilt and shame?

2. Faith come by hearing the Word of Christ Jesus! What could you do to become more aware of the goodness, greatness, and grace of the Lord Jesus in your life?

3. What are the most important "Words of Christ Jesus" that have come to your life? What impact have they had on you?

Personal Journal on this chapter.

For many years I felt I was forgiven by God and even "loved" by. God but not "liked" by God. I felt the Lord tolerated me because of HIS death on the cross but basically was unhappy with me most all the time every day.   It was by reading the book <u>Search for Significance</u> that at a practical and emotional level I began to really believe the gospel of grace that the LORD delighted in me and was rejoicing over me being a part of HIS family.   I had the right theology in my mind about "justification by faith in Jesus Christ" but my heart had not accepted that I was unconditionally fully accepted and embraced by the LORD as a 100% free gift. I felt I had to work and do things to "abide in the vine" instead of knowing that because I knew Jesus as my Lord and Savior, I was already a branch connected to HIM.   I had made "abiding" into a work instead of a reality of God's work in my life.   I had to really believe that "I was clean".

""Abide in Me, and I in you. As the branch cannot bear fruit of itself unless it abides in the vine, so neither can you unless you abide in Me." John 15:4

I am 100% percent dependent on the Vine Jesus to bear spiritual fruit in my life. This is the fruit of the Holy Spirit who is the presence of the Christ Jesus in me. As we have already discovered, the fruit of the Spirit is the love of Jesus Christ given to us in our lives.

"But the fruit of the Spirit is love, joy, peace, patience, kindness, goodness, faithfulness, gentleness, self-control; against such things there is no law. Now those who belong to Christ Jesus have crucified the flesh with its passions and desires. If we live by the Spirit, let us also walk by the Spirit." Galatians 5:22-25

What does it mean to abide, remain, or sojourn in the Vine Jesus?

The Lord Jesus provides us with a bit more insight in these words also found in John's gospel:

"He who eats My flesh and drinks My blood abides in Me, and I in him." John 6:56

In the context of John 6 the eating and drinking of the flesh and blood of the Christ Jesus is to believe in HIM as the Christ, the incarnate Word, and Son of God whose life will be sacrificed as the "Lamb of God" that takes away the sin of the world, most importantly for me, HIS sacrifice takes away my sin.

I am connected to this wonderful sacrificial work by faith in Christ Jesus alone.

"Jesus answered and said to them, "This is the work of God, that you believe in Him whom He has sent."" John 6:29

""Truly, truly, I say to you, he who believes has eternal life." John 6:47

3 "And this is eternal life, that they may know (have a personal intimate relationship) with You, the only true God, and Jesus Christ whom You have sent. [Jhn 17:3 NASB20]

Jesus Christ has given me "eternal Life" which is to be in an intimate personal relationship with the Triune God by having true faith in God's redemptive plan centered in the person of the LORD Jesus. We are now connected, close, and abiding together. HIS life has become my life.

Here Jesus Christ connects this union and communion with the bread and cup of the Lord's supper. Even as the preaching of the gospel and prayer can connect us to the reality of the Living Christ in us, so also the LORD now makes plain that taking the bread and the cup as an act of faith can help us experience the reality of HIS abiding in us.

Now part of my practice as a believer is to receive because of my faith, the communion or Lord's Supper as a way of remembering and participating in the act of salvation that Jesus accomplished by dying for my sin. The Lord gave us the bread and the cup so that we would "remember" or experience again the reality of HIS sacrifice for our sins and resurrection from the dead.

23 For I received from the Lord that which I also delivered to you, that the Lord Jesus in the night in which He was betrayed took bread; 24 and when He had given thanks, He broke it and said, "This is My body, which is for you; do this in remembrance of Me." 25 In the same way [He took] the cup also after supper, saying, "This cup is the new covenant in My blood; do this, as often as you drink [it,] in remembrance of Me." 26 For as often as you eat this bread and drink the cup, you proclaim the Lord's death until He comes. [1Co 11:23-26 NASB95]

The connection between the eating and drinking is part of God's way of us remaining in the VINE Jesus by faith.   God uses the bread and the cup to increase our faith in Christ Jesus. This should be part of our regular corporate worship so that we never forget what Christ Jesus has done.   The taking of the Lord's Supper is one way that my faith increases and my experience of the abiding presence of Christ Jesus grows in my life.

Not only in the taking of communion but part of my abiding in Jesus takes place in my worship of HIM both in private and with others. As I sit at the feet of Jesus, get absorbed in HIS presence, and hear HIS WORD in worship HIS desire to be near me and my desire to be near HIM occurs. Participating in public worship is vital for me to experience the reality of the presence of Christ in me and bearing fruit.

23 "But a time is coming, and even now has arrived, when the true worshipers will worship the Father in spirit and truth; for such people the Father seeks [to be] His worshipers. 24 "God is spirit, and those who worship Him must worship in spirit and truth." [John 4:23-24 NASB20]

23 Let's hold firmly to the confession of our hope without wavering, for He who promised is faithful; 24 and let's consider how to encourage one another in love and good deeds, 25 not abandoning our own meeting together, as is the habit of some people, but encouraging [one another;] and all the more as you see the day drawing near. [Heb 10:23-25 NASB20]

I abide, dwell, and sojourn in the Vine Jesus as I have a relationship of trust in HIM to be my Lord, Savior, Prophet, Priest, and Prince and it is in worship that I can most easily experience the reality of my abiding fellowship with the Lord.

This means that I do not turn away from HIS word or teachings and that I actively focus my faith, trust, gratitude, and loyalty on HIM as my one source of life and love in prayers, singing of songs of faith, prayers, and honest fellowship with other believers where we challenge each other to live in a manner worthy of the gospel of Christ.

Remaining in HIM would normally mean that I am connected to HIS body the Church through participating in loving relationship with other believers and participating in worship with them. The fellowship of believers is "the body of Christ" on the earth and I can see Christ more clearly when I am with other disciples of Jesus doing HIS work and worship in community.

I should seek to have some true "spiritual friends" who I share my life story with, am held accountable for how I live, study scripture with, serve others with, and pray together. The life of Christ is manifested in us as we give ourselves to an honest and real fellowship with one another. The Lord has made our walk with him a "team sport" and there are not to be any "Lone Ranger" Christians.

I want to return to the story we started with concerning Martha and Mary. I think that there is even more in the story to help us understand this part of what it means to abide.

"Now as they were traveling along, He entered a village; and a woman named Martha welcomed Him into her home. She had a sister called Mary, who was seated at the Lord's feet, listening to His word. But Martha was distracted with all her preparations; and she came up to Him and said, "Lord, do You not care that my sister has left me to do all the serving alone? Then tell her to help me." But the Lord answered and said to her, "Martha, Martha, you are worried and bothered about so many things; but only one thing is necessary, for Mary has chosen the good part, which shall not be taken away from her."" Luke 10:38-42

Spending time with the LORD Jesus, resting before HIM, and paying close attention to HIS words is part of the way we abide with HIM and HIS life flows through us bearing the fruit of love (John 15:3).   This should be the focus of our private and public worship of the Lord Jesus. Time of private worship, meditation on scripture, prayer, and praise is a vital part of our lives.

Like Martha, I can become busy with many good things that I think will serve the LORD Jesus but then fail to simply be with HIM to listen to HIM. Our worship of Christ Jesus allows our works to be an expression of the life of Christ in us and not just our own efforts done in our own strength. Now, Martha was also a disciple of the LORD Jesus and had learned from HIM as well as Mary. She had times when she was sitting at HIS feet like Mary. But on that particular day she got distracted by doing things for the Lord instead of focusing on just being with the Lord. [16]

Jesus is telling me that living a life of love, good works, self-denial, and mercy is just a natural process and is as easy and normal as a branch bearing abundant fruit who are attached to a vine. <u>A life of loving good works is the result of having a relationship</u> of living faith with the VINE My faith in Jesus transforms me by dwelling in HIS words, worshipping HIM, and focusing on HIS suffering for my sins to give me forgiveness and eternal life. I have to preach the gospel often to myself if I am to grow in faith and bear abundant loving acts of compassion in my life.

Prayers of faith to Jesus would be part of this abiding. Having honest conversations with the LORD and seeking to hear HIS voice are vital parts of spending time with HIM. The one reality is that I do abide in the VINE Jesus and HE abides with me, but I need to get in touch with this reality in my experience to fully benefit from that reality and to practically bear the fruit of obedient love.

All my effectiveness as a disciple of the Christ Jesus depends on my abiding, remaining, and sojourning with HIM. My success as a follower of Christ Jesus depends on abiding in HIM and will take place because I am "in the VINE". This is the most critical reality to experience in my life. This truth must never be lost in the midst of all our "doing things" for the Lord.

When I spend time in private and public worship, I am sitting at the feet of Jesus and listening to HIS WORD and participating in HIS presence. Times of worship are critical to the "abiding experience" and then lead to a life of service and good works. Doing works without worship will always lead to them being done in our own strength and not in HIS LOVE.

---

[16] The Greek text includes an illuminating variant in v. 39 "[Martha] had a sister called Mary, who **_also_** sat at the Lord's feet."[16]

Prayer

Great Savior, Lord, Prophet, Priest, and Prince Jesus; teach me how to experience and benefit from abiding in YOU. Let me see that without YOU I can do nothing of any worth. So good LORD, who fully understands what it means to abide, please let me become a fruitful branch attached to YOU. I am weak and easily distracted with many things like Martha. Give me the heart of Mary that day that she sat at your feet listening to YOUR words. Please bear your fruit of obedient love through me this day. Without YOU LORD Jesus I can do nothing of any worth this day. Bear YOUR fruit through me. Help me develop a fellowship of "spiritual friends" in whom I can see and experience YOUR life and in this fellowship of love manifest more and more of YOUR love. Amen

Questions

1. Why does it seem we can do many "things" without abiding in the Vine Jesus?

2. How can we overcome the lie that "doing things" is more important than being with the Lord Jesus in fellowship and worship?

3. What step could you take in your relationship with Christ Jesus that would be one in which you feel it would help you experience "abiding".

Personal journal on this chapter: I have found that it is easier for me to get distracted with doing things for the Lord Jesus than actually stopping to be with him. One time I had the deep impression that the Lord wanted me to stop being so busy teaching and counseling so that I could really have a "Sabbath" rest of reflection with HIM. I however kept putting it off. I then became very ill and for the only time in my adult life had to be rushed into the ICU and had to stay there a week recovering. I was put into a private room and the television was not working. Regardless of the medical reasons I was there, I was sure that the heavenly Father was pruning me and making me focus on the Lord. I had access to worship music, scripture, and devotionals on my phone and spent the next week in one of the most intense "spiritual retreats" of my life. During that time, I enjoyed a fellowship with the LORD Jesus that transformed me in many ways. I had sat at the feet of Jesus before this, but like Martha, I had become so focused on doing things for HIM, I had stopped just "being" with HIM..

""I am the vine, you are the branches; he who abides in Me and I in him, he bears much fruit, for apart from Me you can do nothing." John 15:5

Jesus is the vine, the source of life, character, and true effectiveness and I am a believing disciple in union and communion with HIM. HE has placed me into HIM. He has promised me a useful life "in HIM".

""You did not choose Me but I chose you, and appointed you that you would go and bear fruit, and that your fruit would remain, so that whatever you ask of the Father in My name He may give to you. "This I command you, that you love one another." John 15:16-17

I need to moment by moment remain in a trusting relationship of real dependence upon the LORD Jesus the vine. I must recognize that I have no power, life, or ability to bear an effective loving life apart from HIM. I have no ability to produce real good works outside of HIS life flowing through me. Every action of love that I have ever done is really the result of the LORD Jesus' work in me.

When I fail to believe as I should believe, I need to confess my lack of faith, admit that I am trusting in my own righteousness, and focused on selfish ambitions that are keeping me from producing the maximum amount of fruit in my life. The life of faith is one that is lived in constant confession of our sins and our need of the grace of Christ Jesus every second of every day.

8 If we say that we have no sin, we are deceiving ourselves and the truth is not in us. 9 If we confess our sins, He is faithful and righteous to forgive us our sins and to cleanse us from all unrighteousness. 10 If we say that we have not sinned, we make Him a liar and His word is not in us. [1Jo 1:8-10 NASB95]

The hardest sins to repent of is my self-righteousness and self-dependance. My awakening of this truth came as I was involved in a deep study of Christian morals and ethics. I was striving to fully understand what it takes for anything I do to be perfectly right before God. As I studied this, I felt the Lord tell me.

"Norm, I fully love YOU and accept YOU because of what I have done for YOU on the cross. I rejoice that you have a hunger and thirst to understand righteousness. But you must understand that you have never produced even one "micro-second" of life that is perfectly righteous in your own strength"

At that moment I agreed with the prophet Isaiah not just theologically but emotionally and was greatly humbled.

6 For all of us have become like one who is unclean, And all our righteous deeds are like a filthy garment; And all of us wither like a leaf, And our iniquities, like the wind, take us away. [Isa 64:6 NASB95]

Therefore, a life of faith in Christ Jesus as my High Priest and sacrifice for all my sins means that I will live a life of continual confession of my need of HIS forgiving grace. I need amazing grace every "micro-second" of my life until I see HIM face to face and by that vision fully become HIS LOVE incarnate. I am always a work in process.

The more I can really remember and rely on this reality then I can cooperate with this process of bearing the fruit of God's love and love for God in my life by faith, belief, and trust alone.

Even my desire to abide is really the life of Jesus in me producing a hunger and thirst to be in HIM.

I should be in a state of thankfulness and wonder at the heavenly Father and the Son for making this possible. I ought to deeply believe that without the LORD Jesus I can do nothing worth doing for the kingdom of God. My effectiveness is 100% dependent on HIM and HIM alone. This is the truth but I am slow to be fully converted to this truth.

My faith association with the LORD Jesus is then the most critical factor in determining my ability to live a life that has a legacy of loving word, deeds, and attitudes. The more deeply I am "in the vine" and the life of the VINE Jesus flows into me then I will produce an eternally productive way of life day by day. It all depends on my relationship with Christ Jesus. Really knowing HIM is vital.

All my worship, prayer, bible reading, meditation, practicing HIS presence while living and working, needs to be aimed at experiencing the reality of the relationship HE has given me and recognize the wonder of my abiding life that is "IN HIM". To feel HIS life and to allow the flow of HIS life in me to accomplish HIS will on earth as in heaven is really the key to all effective living for HIM.

Prayer

Good, great, and merciful Living Christ Jesus, allow me to be a fruitful branch this day. I don't want to waste today by trying to bear fruit in my own strength. I have no strength. I have no life but the life YOU give me. I am barren and broken outside of YOU. I can produce nothing truly productive outside of YOU. My one hope is that YOUR life will flow through me and produce in me words, actions, and attitudes of LOVE. Regardless of what I do, if I don't have YOUR LOVE in me it profits me nothing at all. LORD, pour out YOUR love into me this day. I cast my many cares on YOU. They are greater than my strength to bear them. Carry them for me. Lift me up, cleanse me, and make me a fruitful branch this day for YOUR glory and my good. Thank YOU for having mercy on me. Amen

Questions – Day 8

1. If all the love you have ever expressed after your acceptance of Christ as Lord and Savior in your life is the fruit of HIS life in you, how does this change how you look at your Christian life?

2. What care and concern do you need to cast on Jesus at this present moment?   Give it to HIM now!

Personal Journal on this chapter – One of the greatest fears I have had since I was a child was the fear of failure. It seemed I would never be strong enough or bright enough to accomplish things and "win" at life.   As I meditated on this passage, I saw that the LORD Jesus had promised me that "in HIM" I could not fail.   HE would produce fruit in my life, make my life fulfill what HE had planned, and accomplish what HE desired to flow out of my life.   I needed to only depend on HIM moment by moment to accomplish HIS purpose for my life.   This new perspective allows me to live a far less stress filled life and in constant fear of failure.

""If anyone does not abide in Me, he is thrown away as a branch and dries up; and they gather them and cast them into the fire and they are burned." John 15:6

There are those who never were in the Vine Jesus and so these are seen as useless branches whose only use is to put into the fire to burn.   Outside of a relationship with Christ Jesus there is no hope to live a successful life. This a sad and frightening reality.

6 Jesus said to him, "I am the way, and the truth, and the life; no one comes to the Father but through Me. [John 14:6 NASB95]

This exclusive certainty is very hard for us to accept because it is hard to believe that outside of a relationship with Christ Jesus, no one produces a life of true LOVE and good deeds.

The Bible's evaluation of our rebellion against the "Kingdom of Love" is very severe and it is why we are in such desperate need of having Jesus Christ be our Lord and Savior. It was only our desperate need that led God to take such desperate action of suffering for our grievous moral depravity so that the forgiveness of our treason against the King of Heaven could be justly given.

9 What then? Are we better than they? Not at all; for we have already charged that both Jews and Greeks are all under sin; 10 as it is written, "THERE IS NONE RIGHTEOUS, NOT EVEN ONE; 11 THERE IS NONE WHO UNDERSTANDS, THERE IS NONE WHO SEEKS FOR GOD; ... 13 "THEIR THROAT IS AN OPEN GRAVE, WITH THEIR TONGUES THEY KEEP DECEIVING," "THE POISON OF ASPS IS UNDER THEIR LIPS"; 14 "WHOSE MOUTH IS FULL OF CURSING AND BITTERNESS"; 15 "THEIR FEET ARE SWIFT TO SHED BLOOD, 16 DESTRUCTION AND MISERY ARE IN THEIR PATHS, 17 AND THE PATH OF PEACE THEY HAVE NOT KNOWN." 18 "THERE IS NO FEAR OF GOD BEFORE THEIR EYES." 19 Now we know that whatever the Law says, it speaks to those who are under the Law, so that every mouth may be closed and all the world may become accountable to God; 20 because by the works of the Law no flesh will be justified in His sight; for through the Law [comes] the knowledge of sin. ... 23 for all have sinned and fall short of the glory of God, [Rom 3:9-11, 13-20, 23 NASB95]

We do not need to worry that any "good person" will be wrongly punished by an all righteous and holy God.   The just and good Creator is not a moral monster who would condemn the innocent. For God is a wise and good judge of all human beings. Indeed, the God of the bible is one who:

8 ... is gracious and compassionate; Slow to anger and great in mercy. [Psa 145:8 NASB20]

13 .... Now return to the LORD your God, For He is gracious and compassionate, Slow to anger, abounding in mercy and relenting of catastrophe. [Joe 2:13 NASB20]

The problem is not with the Creator and moral judge of the universe lacking compassion, character, or competence. Hard for us to believe. The problem is with us.

5 But because of your stubbornness and unrepentant heart you are storing up wrath for yourself in the day of wrath and revelation of the righteous judgment of God, 6 who WILL RENDER TO EACH PERSON ACCORDING TO HIS DEEDS: 7 to those who by perseverance in doing good seek for glory and honor and immortality, eternal life; 8 but to those who are selfishly ambitious and do not obey the truth, but obey unrighteousness, wrath and indignation. 9 [There will be] tribulation and distress for every soul of man who does evil, of the Jew first and also of the Greek, 10 but glory and honor and peace to everyone who does good, to the Jew first and also to the Greek. 11 For there is no partiality with God. [Rom 2:5-11 NASB95]

Those with the Bible will be judged by the Bible and those without the revelation of Scripture will be judged by what they had available to them in general revelation, their own conscience, and reason. God's judgement will be 100% just, fair, and understanding who we are and what we knew. To those that had little, then little will be required and to those who had much revelation and ability, then much will be required.

Dr. Francis Schaeffer once gave an illustration of how this may work. Suppose there was a recording of every moral judgment we made against others as we judged their actions to be lacking love and respect in some way towards us or those we cared about. On the day of judgment this recording is played back, and we are simply judged on the basis that we have judged others. Surely, that would be totally fair.

2 "For in the way you judge, you will be judged; and by your standard of measure, it will be measured to you. [Mat 7:2 NASB20]

The Universal King of reality takes no pleasure in the death and condemnation of human beings yet must uphold the moral and justice of the creation as the Judge of all the earth (Ezekiel 18:32). The punishment that we face will justly fit our true moral guilt. No one will face a punishment after death greater than their crimes. The judge of all the earth will do what is right in every individual case.

The problem is not the justice of God's condemnation of immoral people, but that "there is none righteous" no not one.

It was this horrible reality of our rebellion that demanded that God find a radical solution to our sin problem by having Christ Jesus come to take the penalty of HIS people's sins upon HIMSELF and provide a just way to forgive those who rebelled against HIM and HIS love. We could only be saved by undeserved mercy for all we deserved and had earned was just condemnation.

This is hard for us to accept for we normally think we are better than we really are and have good excuses for all our moral failures. To think that there is such a moral crisis in our lives is very hard for us to fully accept. Most of us don't feel that guilty about how we have lived our lives. This just shows us how seared our conscience is rather than actually being evidence of our righteousness. Accepting the Lord's evaluation of our moral performance is a good place to begin to understand why we so desperately need Jesus Christ to save us.

A book that helped me to deal with the greatness of God's plan of salvation was written by B.B. Warfield and is entitled <u>The Plan of Salvation</u>.[17]   It is a theologically deep work but helped my mind to more fully appreciate the wonder of God's love in Christ Jesus and the goodness of God's answer to the problem of our immoral attitudes, actions, and words.   I highly recommend it for those seeking a better understanding of this deep mystery.

Returning to the passage before us:

 ""If anyone does not abide in Me, he is thrown away as a branch and dries up; and they gather them and cast them into the fire and they are burned." John 15:6 [18]

As we read this passage which records these difficult words from our Lord Jesus it raises the question if some branches who were in the VINE Jesus were "cut off" because they were fruitless (John 15:2). In this case we would have to see the branches as not true believers but those that were formally connected through outward profession to the VINE Jesus, but HIS life was never in them.

The LORD Jesus warns us of such a reality when HE says:

""Not everyone who says to Me, 'Lord, Lord,' will enter the kingdom of heaven, but he who does the will of My Father who is in heaven will enter. "Many will say to Me on that day, 'Lord, Lord, did we not prophesy in Your name, and in Your name cast out demons, and in Your name perform many miracles?' "And then I will declare to them, 'I never knew you; DEPART FROM ME, YOU WHO PRACTICE LAWLESSNESS.'" Matthew 7:21-23

There can be those who profess faith in the LORD Jesus, even do miracles in HIS name, but who never bear the fruit of character transforming love which is the fruit of KNOWING HIM. Their hearts are still lawless and filled with rebellion even when they outwardly preach and minister in the name of Christ Jesus. Without love, nothing they do profits them for they never had a personal relationship with Jesus the LORD. (1 Corinthians 13)

Judas is of course the perfect example of this type of formal relationship which is really without life. Such people do not lose their salvation for Christ Jesus says that he "never knew them". Christ Jesus has taught that HE does not lose any of HIS true sheep. However, there can be "wolves in sheep clothing".

""My sheep hear My voice, and I know them, and they follow Me; and I give eternal life to them, and they will never perish; and no one will snatch them out of My hand. "My Father, who has

---

[17] **The Plan of Salvation** by B. B. Warfield ;
https://www.monergism.com/thethreshold/sdg/pdf/warfield_plan.pdf

[18] Indeed, there is a persistent strand of New Testament witness that depicts men and women with some degree of connection with Jesus, or with the Christian church, who nevertheless by failing to display the grace of perseverance finally testify that the transforming life of Christ has never pulsated within them (*e.g.* Mt. 13:18–23; 24:12; Jn. 8:31ff.; Heb. 3:14–19; 1 Jn. 2:19; 2 Jn. 9).[18] The Gospel of John D,A. Carson)

given them to Me, is greater than all; and no one is able to snatch them out of the Father's hand. "I and the Father are one."" John 10:27-30

Christ Jesus most likely had Ezekiel 15:1-8 in mind as HE taught these words.

"Then the word of the LORD came to me, saying, "Son of man, how is the wood of the vine better than any wood of a branch which is among the trees of the forest? "Can wood be taken from it to make anything, or can men take a peg from it on which to hang any vessel? "If it has been put into the fire for fuel, and the fire has consumed both of its ends and its middle part has been charred, is it then useful for anything? "Behold, while it is intact, it is not made into anything. How much less, when the fire has consumed it and it is charred, can it still be made into anything! "Therefore, thus says the Lord GOD, 'As the wood of the vine among the trees of the forest, which I have given to the fire for fuel, so have I given up the inhabitants of Jerusalem; and I set My face against them. Though they have come out of the fire, yet the fire will consume them. Then you will know that I am the LORD, when I set My face against them. 'Thus, I will make the land desolate, because they have acted unfaithfully,'" declares the Lord GOD." Ezekiel 15:1-8

Jerusalem would again be facing destruction by fire through the Roman armies in 70 A.D. due to their rejection and murder of Christ Jesus. Israel was a branch not attached to the true Vine but thought that their self-righteous religion was the "Vine of God" but it was without life. What happened with the Babylonians will happen again as the legions of Rome destroy Jerusalem because of her sins.   The Lord Jesus' teaching here has both personal and corporate warning to it.

Christ Jesus is teaching clearly that HE is the way, the truth, and the life and no one can be in fellowship with the Father but through HIM (John 14:6).

This seems hard to believe that there is such a narrow way to have eternal life and salvation because we still have faith in our own goodness and righteousness while minimizing our moral guilt.

The reason the only hope is in Christ Jesus, is that we are worst then we think we are and outside of the LORD Jesus we cannot produce any true works of unconditional love. Each of us are radically and massively moral failures every micro-second of our lives.

As we have seen the Apostle Paul teaches reflecting on Psalm 51:1-6 and Psalm 14:1-7 that there are none righteous, pointing us to the reality that without a relationship with Jesus Christ, a person is lost and justly facing condemnation on judgement day. What we have found as we meditated on this passage is because the Lord is just, HE will render to everyone what their lives deserves, but what I deserve justly and rightly is to be thrown as a fruitless branch into the fire of a just and appropriate punishment in hell forever.

This is true of me and of all humanity.

I am in desperate need of a Savior to forgive my sins and a regeneration of my heart that I might produce real words, actions, and attitudes of love. This is our only hope!

The LORD Jesus is that suffering Savior that has paid the price of my moral failures by bearing the just wrath of God for them on the cross and now as the risen LORD and Christ can grant me forgiveness and an abundant life in union and communion with HIM. I can be by HIS grace a fruitful branch sharing HIS LOVE in words and deeds to the entire world.

But outside of a living relationship with Jesus there is only despair, death, and destruction. The most vital issue of my life is "Do I know HIM?" Paul will urge the Corinthian believers to ""Test yourselves to see if you are in the faith; examine yourselves! Or do you not recognize this about yourselves, that Jesus Christ is in you—unless indeed you fail the test?" 2 Corinthians 13:5

It is vital that I test and examine myself to try to ensure my soul that I have a real relationship with the Living Christ Jesus for this is the most critical concern of my eternal soul. The Apostle Paul will tell us:

"Nevertheless, the firm foundation of God stands, having this seal, "The Lord knows those who are His," and, "Everyone who names the name of the Lord is to abstain from wickedness."" 2 Timothy 2:19

While the LORD alone knows exactly who HIS true branches are I can by abstaining from wickedness and seeking to purify myself as HE is pure, demonstrate my living relationship with HIM by faith.   May I keep this reality always fresh in my mind.

Prayer

LORD, let me know the truth as YOU know the truth. I don't want to just imagine that I abide in YOU while the truth is that I am cut off, fruitless, and damned. Assure me through YOUR SPIRIT within me and by bearing fruit through me that I am "IN YOU". Lord cleanse me and help be bear more abundant fruit today. Maximize my ability to produce words and actions of YOUR perfect love in my life. Allow me to reach my full potential for YOU and YOUR kingdom. Amen

Questions – Day nine

1. Do you have a living relationship with the Living Christ Jesus? Why do you believe this is true?

2. Some Christians are too quick to claim the Lord Jesus as "fire insurance" and live for the devil while claiming heaven as their home and others are too quick to doubt their relationship with the LORD Jesus, causing them to despair instead of hope.

How would you keep yourself free of both extremes?

Personal Journal on this chapter: I got my original theological training from people who taught an "easy believism" that did not require accepting Christ Jesus as the "Lord" or any repentance of sin. One could simply take Jesus as eternal life insurance by believing you were saved by "grace" alone and live all your days in moral and selfish immorality.   But as I studied the Scripture and grew in my relationship with the LORD Jesus this clearly was not what was being taught in the Bible. For while we were fully saved by grace alone, this living grace always brought about a substantial change in the lives of those who had a real relationship with the LORD.   As I came to understand that the title "Christ" really meant "Messiah" or the ultimate anointed Prophet, Priest and Prince of God then accepting the Lord Jesus meant I had to trust in HIM to teach me the truth, be the full payment of my sins, and the ruler of my life.   I could not accept HIM as my "Priest" but reject HIM as my Prophet and Prince.   I had to accept all of Jesus Christ or reject all that HE is in my life. This radically changed my ideas on what it meant to be a believer.

""If you abide in Me, and My words abide in you, ask whatever you wish, and it will be done for you." John 15:7

This abiding, remaining, and sojourning in the VINE Jesus is connected to HIS words remaining in us. This would imply that one of the ways that I am connected to the Living Lord Jesus is through HIS words which are found in the gospels and the whole revelation of the Bible. Part of being a believing disciple is the desire to master and be mastered by the words of my Master Jesus.

What does it mean to be a believing disciple?

"Typically in the Jewish world, a disciple would voluntarily join a school or otherwise seek out a master rabbi; however, Jesus seeks out and chooses those whom HE wants as HIS disciples (Mk 1:17; 2:14; Lk 5:1–11; cf. Mt 4:18–21). A dedicated disciple was generally expected someday to become a rabbi himself, yet Jesus teaches his disciples that HE will always be their rabbi and they will have a lifetime of discipleship (Mt 23:8; cf. Mt 10:24–25, 37; Lk 14:26–27; Jn 11:16). Jesus' disciples are bound to HIM and to God's will (Mt 12:46–50; cf. Mk 3:31–45). They are called to a lifetime of work and service (Mt 16:15–19; Mk 1:17; Lk 5:10)," (Mounce's Complete Expository Dictionary of Old & New Testament words: Zondervan)

A disciple was one who had found a "master teacher"; who one was so awed by their lives and wisdom that they wanted to think, feel, and act as a clone of that person. There was a deep admiration, love, devotion, and following of this teacher. In Jesus' case HE chose those who would be HIS most intimate followers and they responded to this call by following, learning, and striving to imitate HIM. There was a deep love between the "master teacher" and his students.

Abiding in the LORD Jesus, is actively engaging in the teachings and life of HIM so that they saturate my head, govern my heart, and guide my hands in all that I do. It is to have the life teachings of Jesus empowered by the Holy Spirit deeply abide in my soul so that out of these words of Jesus, my world view, attitudes, goals, hopes, and dreams are created.

John Piper says:

"What that means for letting the words of Jesus abide in us is that we do not just read the Bible, and do not just memorize and meditate on the Bible, and do not just listen to preaching and teaching from the Bible. It means that we seek the words of Jesus as living words — words that come not in the abstract but come from the heart and on the lips of a living Person whom we love more than any other person in the world."[19]

At this point the LORD Jesus gives an astonishing promise that the disciple who is so dominated by HIS words can ask whatever they wish in prayer, and it will be done for them. He had said this earlier.

---

[19] https://www.desiringgod.org/messages/if-my-words-abide-in-you

""Whatever you ask in My name, that will I do, so that the Father may be glorified in the Son. "If you ask Me anything in My name, I will do it." John 14:13-14

<u>Now to ask in the "name" of the LORD Jesus is to make our prayers by HIS authority, for HIS purposes, and for HIS pleasure.</u>

Whatever I ask for the will of the LORD Jesus to be done on earth as in heaven by HIS authority as King of kings, will be done since my prayers are now the echoes of HIS heart.

<u>In the context of John 15 it would be prayers to bear the fruit of love in every relationship in my life and to have the wisdom of Christ Jesus totally dominate my thoughts, attitudes, and actions.</u> Such a promise is not to be used for my selfish desires but for HIS kingdom desires in my life and the lives of others. If I pray to overflow with more of HIS unconditional love because of HIS life in me, such a prayer will be answered.

My prayers are focused on bearing "Jesus' fruit" if I am abiding in HIM and HIS WORD.   Such prayers will be answered. They are "Kingdom Focused Prayers" and deeply informed prayers guided by the wisdom and life of my Master Jesus and guided by the HOLY SPIRIT. [20]

Prayer

Great Redeeming Creator in Christ Jesus, put in me a deeper awe of YOUR greatness, goodness, and grace. Open my mind and heart to YOUR WORDS Christ. Let them deeply abide in my inner core and soul. Allow them to guide my petitions and desires. Allow me now to pray the prayers that will allow fruit to be released in my life.   Forgive me for thinking I don't need YOUR WORDS but only my own words to govern my head, heart, and hands. Forgive my pride, rebellion, and independent attitude. Help me to see that without YOU and YOUR WORDS, I can do nothing that matters or will last. Help me to have a humble, submissive, and dependent attitude that relies and rests in YOU moment by moment. Amen

---

[20] Understanding unanswered prayers is important.   I would recommend The Prayer Course II at https://unanswered.prayercourse.org/ by Peter Greig and his book <u>God on Mute</u>.

Questions for Chapter Ten – Day 10

1. How would having "Kingdom Focused" prayers change the way you pray?

2. What "Kingdom Focused" prayer is the Lord leading you to pray today?

Personal Journal on this chapter

I have found focusing my prayers on the priority of bearing the fruit of the Spirit which is LOVE very difficult because here "East of Eden" there are so many great needs, struggles, pains, fears, losses, and struggles. I take comfort in the disciple's prayer that Jesus Christ taught us to pray since it opens the door to my wrestling with all the dynamics of the difficult lives we must live till the kingdom of LOVE is fully realized and manifested. I find myself still striving to understand how to consistently have "abiding prayer" and am thankful for God's grace in teaching me how to pray.

26 Now in the same way the Spirit also helps our weakness; for we do not know what to pray for as we should, but the Spirit Himself intercedes for [us] with groanings too deep for words; 27 and He who searches the hearts knows what the mind of the Spirit is, because He intercedes for the saints according to [the will of] God. [Rom 8:26-27 NASB20]

9 "Pray, then, in this way: 'Our Father, who is in heaven, Hallowed be Your name. 10 'Your kingdom come. Your will be done, On earth as it is in heaven. 11 'Give us this day our daily bread. 12 'And forgive us our debts, as we also have forgiven our debtors. 13 'And do not lead us into temptation, but deliver us from evil.' [Mat 6:9-13 NASB20][21]

---

[21] A book worth reading on prayer. **How to Pray: A Simple Guide for Normal People**
by Pete Greig and the Prayer Course 1 found at https://prayercourse.org/sessions/

""My Father is glorified by this, that you bear much fruit, and so prove to be My disciples." John 15:8

The heavenly Father's goodness, greatness, and grace is proclaimed and manifested before all creation when the life of the VINE Jesus flows into believing disciples and they bear the fruit of lives filled with actions, attitudes, and words of true love.

The ultimate evidence that I truly have become a disciple of the LORD Jesus with a living relationship with HIM is when HIS unconditional and sacrificial love for others is seen in me (John 15:12).

The purpose of my life is to reflect the character, competence, and compassion of the God as manifested in the Lord Jesus Christ.

As I become an imitator of HIM by having HIS life flow into me and bear fruit through me, I reach the full potential of my life.

This is a far cry from the purpose of my life is to find personal peace and prosperity since to love as the Lord Jesus loved means that I will have to sacrifice my personal peace and prosperity for the good of others and HIS kingdom. I will have to take up my cross and follow HIM.

I am tempted many times to live for my own glory and not to see the Father be glorified in me. I want my goodness, my greatness, and my grace proclaimed. I don't want my good deeds seen as the life of Christ Jesus in me but as a demonstration that I am better and brighter than others. I want to build my own ego through acts of self-righteousness instead of having Christ's righteousness flowing through me that people might see my good works so that they may give glory to my Father in heaven.

As Jesus taught in the Sermon on the Mount; ""Let your light shine before men in such a way that they may see your good works and glorify your Father who is in heaven." Matthew 5:16

When I was in Bible college a few of us came to the realization that the purpose of life was to "glorify God" and not just to "win souls".

Our school's one focus was just on seeing people become believers so that they could go to heaven. We were spiritual "fire rescue people" who were snatching people out of the flames by preaching the gospel of grace to them. The only thing that mattered is that they become "believers in grace" that they might escape hell fire. Now my school had little vision of really making them disciples except that they also could become "fire rescue people". The focus was a spiritual type of humanitarianism and not about the greatness, goodness, and grace of the heavenly Father being seen before a watching world.

As we read passages from Paul; "Whether, then, you eat or drink or whatever you do, do all to the glory of God." 1 Corinthians 10:31. We could see that our only concern should not just be evangelism but to "glorify God".

Yet this truth just became for me evidence that I was "better and brighter" than those who were "fire rescue" Christians. I had become part of an elite group of those who knew the real purpose of was to "glorify God" and this became a source of self-righteousness and pride in me instead of a revelation of the goodness, greatness, and grace of God.   So instead of this truth leading to the glory of God it led to me glorifying myself for having greater knowledge than other people.

It is so easy to even have truth misused in my life.

As Pastor John Piper says; "We live to make Christ look magnificent!" As John the Baptist said must be true of my life; "HE must increase but I must decrease" (John 3:30). On the day of judgment, the LORD will not be focused on how much we knew but on how well we had shown our love for HIM by demonstrating HIS love to others.

""But when the Son of Man comes in His glory, and all the angels with Him, then He will sit on His glorious throne. "All the nations will be gathered before Him; and He will separate them from one another, as the shepherd separates the sheep from the goats; and He will put the sheep on His right, and the goats on the left. "Then the King will say to those on His right, 'Come, you who are blessed of My Father, inherit the kingdom prepared for you from the foundation of the world. 'For I was hungry, and you gave Me something to eat; I was thirsty, and you gave Me something to drink; I was a stranger, and you invited Me in; naked, and you clothed Me; I was sick, and you visited Me; I was in prison, and you came to Me.' "Then the righteous will answer Him, 'Lord, when did we see You hungry, and feed You, or thirsty, and give You something to drink? 'And when did we see You a stranger, and invite You in, or naked, and clothe You? 'When did we see You sick, or in prison, and come to You?' "The King will answer and say to them, 'Truly I say to you, to the extent that you did it to one of these brothers of Mine, even the least of them, you did it to Me.' "Then He will also say to those on His left, 'Depart from Me, accursed ones, into the eternal fire which has been prepared for the devil and his angels; for I was hungry, and you gave Me nothing to eat; I was thirsty, and you gave Me nothing to drink; I was a stranger, and you did not invite Me in; naked, and you did not clothe Me; sick, and in prison, and you did not visit Me.' "Then they themselves also will answer, 'Lord, when did we see You hungry, or thirsty, or a stranger, or naked, or sick, or in prison, and did not take care of You?'"Then He will answer them, 'Truly I say to you, to the extent that you did not do it to one of the least of these, you did not do it to Me.' "These will go away into eternal punishment, but the righteous into eternal life."" Matthew 25:31-46

The evidence that I am a true disciple is not in the "rightness" of my doctrinal statements and creeds but in the demonstration of Christ's love overflowing out of me. Having right biblical doctrine is important, but much more important is having "right" divine LOVE flowing out of me.

34 "I am giving you a new commandment, that you love one another; just as I have loved you, that you also love one another. 35 "By this all [people] will know that you are My disciples: if you have love for one another." [Jhn 13:34-35 NASB20]

Now none of us will love perfectly. We must be in a continual confession of our failure to love as we ought to love. Yet our connection with the life of Christ should manifest itself in a substantial expression of love in a practical way. Even my confession of my failure to love is the fruit of Christ's love in me for it demonstrates humility and the need I have of Christ loving through me.

To really be a true disciple I have to have deeds of love which comes from the abiding life of the VINE Jesus flow into me and out of me for the purpose of all creation seeing reflected in me the goodness, greatness, and grace of the heavenly Father. I cannot do this perfectly, but it can be experienced in a real way. This is why I was, born and reborn. This is supposed to be the ultimate concern of my life, to see the heavenly Father glorified by manifesting the love of Christ overflowing out of me.

Prayer

Good, great, and merciful Father in heaven who has brought infinite grace to me in my Christ Jesus, forgive me for my pride, self-centeredness, and spiritual blindness. Forgive me for even turning truth into something that serves me, to exalt me, instead of serving YOU. Give to me the gift of humility. Save me from my pride. For YOUR glory save me from myself.

Broken as I am, still allow YOUR life LORD Jesus to come flowing through me. Good Father prune me that I will bear more fruit. Allow me to be a true branch with true union with YOU and bring acts of love through me that the Father might be glorified in some ways through the tangled messy life I live.

LORD, have mercy, lift me up, cleanse me, and make me a fruitful branch. Amen

Chapter Eleven Questions. – Day 11

1. Do you live to have people see the "glory of the gospel" in your daily attitudes, words, and actions by having the life of Christ flow through you? Is this part of your daily and normal approach to daily life?   Explain your answer.

2. How would you define success?   Do you think that your definition is the same as God has for your life?

Personal Journal on this chapter - I began my service for the Lord Jesus really as a "Christian humanitarian" in which my main focus was on the need of people to be saved and Christ Jesus was just a "means" through which that could be accomplished.   I saw the need of people to have spiritual and moral awakening for their sakes and the sake of others that they impacted.   I even could see Christ Jesus as a means of changing society and culture bringing much good to societies.   But to actually show love to others so that God the Father and the Lord Jesus would be glorified was something that has been a long journey for me.   I needed to see that the glory of God was really the "end" and not a means just to help people. To have concern about God's reputation of being manifested as good, great, and gracious because I cared about HIM and not because HE was a means of helping people. Yet, this is really what the life of Christ is all about in me. For all the Son did HE did for the glory of the Father in heaven.   To actually do all things so that God will be honored, respected, revealed, and glorified means that I love HIM more than just what he can do to help people,

Practical Tools for Abiding in Christ

This chapter is a practical process that I developed for my own times of abiding with the Lord Jesus. It is my way of doing "Private Worship". If you can do this daily, it would be wonderful but even if you did it weekly or monthly, I think it could be a means of seeking to experience the reality of the life of the VINE that is in us. Some dedicate a weekend retreat to using this process to seek a deeper "abiding experience" with the Lord. I find it very useful in my life and therefore I share it with you in the hope of it being of help to you. On this day try to do as least some of this process in prayer.

The Seven Rs and Seven Kingdom Prayers

Spend two minutes in silence before the presence of the Living Christ and ask HIM to reveal himself to you. Listen to some hymns or praise songs especially those that help you sense the presence of the Lord.

1. <u>Request</u> the Seven Kingdom Prayer

    a. Give me good soil in my heart that I may bear your fruit (Matthew 13:23).
    b. Give me the gift of faith to believe in Lord Jesus as a true disciple (Romans 10:17).
    c. Give me a changed renewed mind that can think Jesus' thoughts after HIM and reject the thoughts of the unbelieving culture in which I was raised (Romans 12:1-3)
    d. Let not my will but YOUR will be done in my life. (Luke 22:42)
    e. Fill me with the Holy Spirit that I may be controlled by the Holy Spirit and filled with divine love through HIM (Romans 5:1-5; Ephesians 5:17-21)
    f. Let me abide in the Vine Jesus as a branch and bear much fruit. (John 15:1-8)
    g. Deliver me from the evil one, the world, and my own unbelief. Defeat the purpose of the devil in my life. (Matthew 6:13)

2. <u>Review</u> the last twenty-four hours if done daily. The last week if done weekly. The last month if done monthly,

    a. What good did the Lord bring into your life and what good did you bring to the lives of others?
    b. What bad things happened in your life? How did you see the Lord working even through loss, pain, abuse, and suffering?
    c. What ugly actions, words, or attitudes did you have in the last twenty-four hours. Where did you hurt or sin against others?
    d. Where did you most see Jesus active in the last twenty-four hours? Did Jesus disappoint you today in some way? What questions do you have for Jesus? What praise could you give Jesus.

3. <u>Repent</u> – Confess to God the ugly things you have done, accept HIS forgiveness in Christ Jesus, and seek to turn away from these sins. Ask yourself, "Why did I do this?" or "What caused me to act this way". Confess these root attitudes as well as the actual sin. (1 John 1:8-10)

4. Rejoice – Look at the good you received as the gift of God to you through others and the good you did to others as the life of Christ being released through you. Praise God for HIS blessing you in these ways,

5. Release – Cast all your cares of the day upon the Lord for the LORD Jesus cares for you and loves you. Look to the day coming up and give it to God, surrendering each event and saying, "not my will but your will be done." (1 Peter 5:7; James 4:15)

6. Read – Take time to meditate upon a paragraph of scripture, a portion of a psalm, or some short segment that you can deeply meditate upon. This would be a "Sacred Reading" of scripture as we did with John 15:1-8.

> 1. Read it out loud and ask the Holy Spirit to speak to you through the passage.
>
> 2. Paraphrase the scripture in your own words and read this out loud. Ask the Holy Spirit to speak to you through this passage.
>
> 3. What is God specifically saying to you in this passage today? What words or phrases most strike you? Put your name in the passage and read it with your name put into the verse so that God is speaking to you. Pray the Holy Spirit to speak to you through the Word.
>
> 4. Read the passage out loud and ask the Lord how you are to apply it. Write out the application. Commit this to God in prayer.

7. Rest in the Lord – Sing a song to the Lord and just be with HIM for a time. End in at least two minutes of silence open to be led by the Lord's Spirit.

Prayer: Lord use this process to help deepen our awareness of YOUR presence, peace, and power in our lives. Use this process as a sincere way to seek YOUR face. Amen

Questions

What made the "Seven Rs' helpful to you? Why?

What was the least effective part of this process?   Why?

Personal Journal for this chapter

I have attempted to use a wide range of various approaches in seeking to experience the abiding presence of the Lord in my life. The "Seven Rs" is a process I developed by studying various traditions of people who used these practices in seeking an encounter with the Living Christ. It has become a habit that is nearly daily in my life although I also change things up at times to keep myself from falling into an empty ritual. Regardless of what we do, keeping things simple, real, and regular is vital as we spend time with the LORD.

Chapter Thirteen - Adapting "Abiding to different personalities, cultures, and people

One problem with this issue of "Abiding" is that it can seem that it favors people who are introverts over people who are extroverts. Many would look at my idea of the "Seven Rs" as just not the way they are wired.

I am aware that because I am an extreme introvert this book may be prejudiced for people who more naturally follow Mary's approach to spirituality instead of Martha's walk with the Lord. Therefore, I wanted to provide help to everyone to be aware of the wide range of ways we can seek to experience the abiding relationship we have been given in Christ Jesus.

A book I found very helpful in solving this problem was <u>Sacred Pathways</u> by Gary Thomas in which he connects the idea of "abiding with Christ" with various personality types. He believes there are nine pathways that Christians have found helpful as they seek to experience the life of the VINE in a practical way in their lives.   This book had a profound impact on me and I highly recommend people reading it.

I want to introduce this idea to you so that you can experiment with various other ways of seeking to experience the presence of the life of Christ beyond what I have focused on in this book. This is here especially for those who have felt frustrated because you having, a "devotional time" has not helped you to really find spiritual reality in your relationship with Christ Jesus.

I have renamed some of the different approaches to seeking the abiding experience from what is found in the book <u>Sacred Pathways</u> because I wanted to simplify these approaches the best I could here but highly recommend you read the book for yourself.

Now for each of these approaches the danger is that they will become idols instead of doorways leading to the living Christ. Whatever means we use to seek the LORD Jesus there is always the danger that the "means" becomes the "end" and we stop seeking to know the person of Christ Jesus and only value a particular experience. But understand whatever process we use, the danger of making it an idol remains and this is an issue of the heart not of a particular process.

1. Experiencing the Abiding in Christ as the Creator – The Naturalist

1 In the beginning was the Word, and the Word was with God, and the Word was God. 2 He was in the beginning with God. 3 All things came into being through Him, and apart from Him not even one thing came into being that has come into being. [Jhn 1:1-3 NASB20]

There are two books written by God to reveal Christ. One is the written WORD and the other is all of creation. Nature is a revelation of the LORD Jesus and reveals to us HIS presence, power, and wisdom. Many people become more aware of being "in the vine" during a walk in the woods or watching the ocean toss than they do in any other way. If this is a practice that impacts your emotions and heart then set aside "sacred space" in your life to simply seek the abiding presence of Christ by seeing, hearing, and touching HIS creation.

2. Experiencing the Abiding in Christ through the beauty and art of historic Christian culture –
Sensates & Traditionalist – I combine two of Gary Thomas' groups into one here.

2 Now I praise you because you remember me in everything and hold firmly to the traditions, just as
I handed them down to you. [1Co 11:2 NASB20]

15 So then, brothers [and sisters,] stand firm and hold on to the traditions which you were taught,
whether by word [of mouth] or by letter from us. [2Th 2:15 NASB20]

For some who have been raised in Christian culture or who want to feel the weight of a faith that
now is 2000 years old there is an awareness of the presence, power, and peace of the life of Christ
awakened by exposure to ancient expressions of faith, works of art that are glorifying to God,
classical hymns, music, and that which connects them to the Christ of history. Having regular
practices and structure to their private and public worship helps them connect with the life of Christ
in them.

Now for some people we would want to reject this as a legitimate way to have the "abiding
experience" but this may be due to our failure to see how many "ward robes" the merciful Father
has provided for his very diverse children to enter into the life of the VINE. There can also be
seasons in our lives where we need to connect with the life of Christ in us in different ways.

Peter Greig, found of the 24/7 prayer movement shares one of his experiences in finding the
presence of Christ in an unexpected way during a time of spiritual crisis in his life.

"There was a season of my life when I just couldn't face attending the kind of freestyling
charismatic worship service my own church was serving up at that time. Sammy (his wife) was
incredibly unwell, and my heart was simply too vulnerable to run the gauntlet of spontaneity every
week. And so I found myself rising early on Sundays to sneak away to our local Anglican cathedral
for a short, anonymous service of Holy Communion in that great fan-vaulted, ancient barn. I hoped
no one would recognize me. I was meant to be leading one of the wildest, most charismatic, least
traditional congregations in town. After the services, I would sometimes pull a hoodie over my head
as if I were leaving a strip club rather than a cathedral. I was embarrassed to find myself sampling
and even appreciating the kind of liturgy we had often denounced as "dead religion" or "vain
repetition." And yet I kept returning for several months because I valued the way that every word of
every service in this ancient building seemed to matter. Nothing was left to chance. When your soul
is spent and you've run out of imagination and initiative, it's a relief to be told what to say by
someone you trust. I also appreciated the sense of being part of something very old—bigger than
my own chaotic predicament and stronger than my own brittle resolve. It was a relief to be sedated
by the predictability of the lectionary, the serene circadian cycles of ecclesiastical routine."[22]

Pastor Greig here shows how we may have to seek new ways to abide in Christ at different times in
our lives. If for whatever reason connecting with the historic cultural expressions of Christ helps
you have a sense of HIM then this may prove useful as you seek to bear "much fruit for HIS glory".

---

[22] Greig, Pete. How to Pray: A Simple Guide for Normal People (pp. 62-63). The Navigators. Kindle Edition.

3. Experiencing the Abiding in Christ in solitude, simplicity, with a focus on personal relationship alone – The Ascetics and Contemplatives – I again combine two of Gary Thomas's categories

9 I, John, your brother and fellow participant in the tribulation and kingdom and perseverance in Jesus, was on the island called Patmos because of the word of God and the testimony of Jesus. 10 I was in [the] Spirit on the Lord's day, and I heard behind me a loud voice like [the sound] of a trumpet, [Rev 1:9-10 NASB20]

35 And in the early morning, while it was still dark, Jesus got up, left [the house,] and went away to a secluded place, and prayed there [for a time.] [Mar 1:35 NASB20]

2 The Bride "May he kiss me with the kisses of his mouth! For your love is sweeter than wine. 3 "Your oils have a pleasing fragrance, Your name is [like] purified oil; Therefore the young women love you. 4 "Draw me after you [and] let's run [together!] The king has brought me into his chambers." The Chorus "We will rejoice in you and be joyful; We will praise your love more than wine. Rightly do they love you." [Sng 1:2-4 NASB20]

31 FOR THIS REASON A MAN SHALL LEAVE HIS FATHER AND HIS MOTHER AND BE JOINED TO HIS WIFE, AND THE TWO SHALL BECOME ONE FLESH. 32 This mystery is great; but I am speaking with reference to Christ and the church. [Eph 5:31-32 NASB20]

Some people feel closest to the reality of the life of Christ within them by being totally alone in times of prayer, journaling, and meditation on scripture. Rather than feeling the presence of Christ in public worship, loud music, or interactions with people, for these people the life of Christ in them becomes most experienced when they are alone with the Lord. Experiencing the Abiding in Christ is a personal intimate private experience with Christ and focus on HIS Love for them and their love for HIM.

There may also be here the entering into the lamentations of Christ over a broken world and unfaithful church.   There is not just the experience of God's redemptive love but a sharing in HIS broken heart over the sorrow of a "East of Eden" world.   This is a fellowship in the sorrow of Christ.   Learning to express and write personal lamentations can be a significant part of this tradition. [23]

Fellowship with the Living Christ sometimes will lead us into the Garden of Gethsemane.

4. Experiencing the Abiding in Christ by confessing Christ boldly – Activist

---

[23] Learning how to lament is found here: https://bridgewayresources.church/how-to-write-your-own-lament-2/#:~:text=%20There%20are%20several%20ways%20you%20can%20go,your%20guide%2C%20write%20your%20own%20words...%20More%20

1 Now in those days John the Baptist came, preaching in the wilderness of Judea, saying, 2 "Repent, for the kingdom of heaven is at hand." ... 7 But when he saw many of the Pharisees and Sadducees coming for baptism, he said to them, "You offspring of vipers, who warned you to flee from the wrath to come? 8 "Therefore produce fruit consistent with repentance; 9 and do not assume that you can say to yourselves, 'We have Abraham [as our] father'; for I tell you that God is able, from these stones, to raise up children for Abraham. 10 "And the axe is already laid at the root of the trees; therefore, every tree that does not bear good fruit is being cut down and thrown into the fire. [Mat 3:1-2, 7-10 NASB20]

Some people feel the living presence of Christ most when they are standing for Christ in either evangelism or calling society to repentance.   They are "filled with the Holy Spirit" and this leads them to pronounce the gospel boldly even being willing to be persecuted for their faith.   At such moments, some disciples feel the closest fellowship with the living presence, power, and peace of the Lord Jesus.

5. Experiencing the Abiding in Christ by acts of compassion to others – Caregivers

9 Be hospitable to one another without complaint. 10 As each one has received a [special] gift, employ it in serving one another as good stewards of the multifaceted grace of God. 11 Whoever speaks [is to do so] as [one who is speaking] actual words of God; whoever serves [is to do so] as [one who is serving] by the strength which God supplies; so that in all things God may be glorified through Jesus Christ, to whom belongs the glory and dominion forever and ever. Amen. [1Pe 4:9-11 NASB20]

Some believers express the Love of Christ overflowing through them most when they are in the actual service of caring for the sick, visiting the prisoners, counseling the depressed, feeding the poor, and befriending the lonely.   In the actual actions of loving others, they experience the reality of the abiding presence of the living Christ within them.

6. Experiencing the Abiding in Christ in free and focused corporate worship – Enthusiasts

1 Praise the LORD! Praise God in His sanctuary; Praise Him in His mighty expanse. 2 Praise Him for His mighty deeds; Praise Him according to His excellent greatness. 3 Praise Him with trumpet sound; Praise Him with harp and lyre. 4 Praise Him with tambourine and dancing; Praise Him with stringed instruments and flute. 5 Praise Him with loud cymbals; Praise Him with resounding cymbals. 6 Everything that has breath shall praise the LORD. Praise the LORD! [Psa 150:1-6 NASB20]

Some brothers and sisters in Christ experience the living presence of Christ most in dynamic fellowship with other believers in joyful celebration of the gospel and love of God in group worship times. They seek to experience the abiding life of Christ in excited worship and focus upon the victory of Christ over the world, the flesh, and the devil.

7. Experiencing the Abiding of Christ by Loving God with all the mind – Intellectuals

37 And He said to him, "'YOU SHALL LOVE THE LORD YOUR GOD WITH ALL YOUR HEART, AND WITH ALL YOUR SOUL, AND WITH ALL YOUR MIND.' [Mat 22:37 NASB20]

Some believers have their most profound and life changing experience of the life of Christ as they diligently study the scripture, philosophy, science, history, physics, music, art and theology.   In the midst of their pondering and praying they gain new revelation about the work and wisdom of Christ and share in thinking HIS thoughts after HIM and being transformed by a powerful revelation that comes through the process of intellectual focus, discipline, and seeking for TRUTH.

Gary Thomas suggests that some of these approaches may come more naturally to us and especially during times of spiritual dryness it may be good to try a different approach as we seek revival and renewal of our faith.   I highly recommend you get the book <u>Sacred Pathways</u> and seek to apply into your life since it has helped me to have a fuller understanding of how disciples of Jesus experience HIS life in them. [24]

I am not suggesting that this is any type of exhaustive list of "doorways" to enter into the reality of. the life of Christ that is in us. Ask the Lord to lead you into the path in which YOU will bear the most love for HIS glory. I am suggesting that Christ Jesus is very creative and has developed a way for every one of HIS children to enjoy fellowship with HIM that fits exactly who HE made them to be.

Prayer: Lord Jesus YOU know me so please let me find the most effective process of bearing abundant fruit from YOUR life overflowing out of me.   Open the doors that I need opened to bear more of the fruit of love for YOUR glory. Amen

Journaling on Chapter Thirteen - Day 13

---

[24] A study guide for **Sacred Pathways** the book by Gary Thomas. https://garythomas.com/wp-content/uploads/2013/02/sacredpathways.pdf

1. Which of the different approaches to experiencing the abiding presence of Christ have you found most effective in your walk of faith.

2. Which ones do you have the least faith would be of help to you? Why

Personal Journaling - I have normally summarized who I am as a "rational mystic". The times that have had the greatest impact in my life is during time of solitude and simplicity where I am just seeking to connect with the presence of Christ within me alone and also as I do research, writing, and study that becomes a significant encounter with the Lord. I think that all of my intellectual pursuits need to be done in an attitude of prayer encounter with Jesus Christ. At various times almost all of the different sacred pathways have been used in my life. I urge you to seek to be creative and open to what the LORD may use to have you overflow with HIS loving presence in YOUR life.

Now we always want to limit our experiences to what is biblically sound and true to the WORD. The Scriptures must guide us and all of our seeing of the LORD Jesus needs to be done within the limits of true faith as taught in the scriptures. While there is freedom there is also form as we seek to know the true living Christ within us.

1 It was for freedom that Christ set us free; therefore keep standing firm and do not be subject again to a yoke of slavery. ... 13 For you were called to freedom, brothers [and sisters;] only [do] not [turn] your freedom into an opportunity for the flesh, but serve one another through love. [Gal 5:1, 13 NASB20]

Chapter Fourteen – Why this Waste? Another story about Mary – Day 14

1 Therefore, six days before the Passover, Jesus came to Bethany where Lazarus was, whom Jesus had raised from the dead. 2 So they made Him a dinner there, and Martha was serving; and Lazarus was one of those reclining [at the table] with Him. 3 Mary then took a pound of very expensive perfume of pure nard, and anointed the feet (and the head – Mark 14:3) of Jesus and wiped His feet with her hair; and the house was filled with the fragrance of the perfume. 4 But Judas Iscariot, one of His disciples, the one who intended to betray Him, said, 5 "Why was this perfume not sold for three hundred denarii ($27,000 in 2022) and [the proceeds] given to poor [people?]" 6 Now he said this, not because he cared about the poor, but because he was a thief, and as he kept the money box, he used to steal from what was put into it. 7 Therefore Jesus said, "Leave her alone, so that she may keep it for the day of My burial. 8 "For you always have the poor with you, but you do not always have Me." [John 12:1-8 NASB20]

3 While He was in Bethany at the home of Simon the leper, and reclining [at the table,] there came a woman with an alabaster vial of very costly perfume of pure nard; [and] she broke the vial and poured it over His head. 4 But some were indignantly [remarking] to one another, "Why has this perfume been wasted? 5 "For this perfume might have been sold for over three hundred denarii, and [the money] given to the poor." And they were scolding her. 6 But Jesus said, "Let her alone; why do you bother her? She has done a good deed to Me. 7 "For you always have the poor with you, and whenever you wish you can do good to them; but you do not always have Me. 8 "She has done what she could; she has anointed My body beforehand for the burial. 9 "Truly I say to you, wherever the gospel is preached in the whole world, what this woman has done will also be spoken of in memory of her." [Mar 14:3-9 NASB95]

The exact sequence of events that led up to this interaction between Mary and Jesus is open to debate, but in John's focus following Lazarus being raised from the dead (John 11) there is a dinner in which the now living Lazarus and the Lord Jesus are at a celebration dinner. This occurs six days before the Passover which would be the time of Christ Jesus' crucifixion and we see Mary again at the feet of Jesus, but now in an act of submission, adoration, and radical worship.

Mary will pour 11.5 ounces of expensive perfume on the feet of Jesus. Guests were served from the inside of the triclinium (a dining table with couches along three sides), but Mary came around the outside and therefore could pour her perfume over Jesus' feet which we extended outward away from the table and she also anointed his head with perfume which filled the whole house with the sweet smell.

This represented a "family treasure" and could well have been part of the retirement funds that Mary might need when she became older. From a human point of view, it was an extravagant and radical action she took. First, the washing of feet was seen as a humiliating act even for slaves to be asked to do and in Jewish culture a woman's long hair was regarded as her glory (1 Cor. 11:15; cf. 1 Pet. 3:3) and therefore this is an act of ultimate devotion, submission, and honor. [25]

Yet, it must be remembered, the Lord Jesus was sitting at the table with her brother who HE had just raised from the dead.   He had turned a day of mourning into a day of rejoicing and demonstrated that HE was the resurrection and the life.

[25] Colin G. Kruse, John: An Introduction and Commentary, ed. Eckhard J. Schnabel, Second edition., vol. 4, Tyndale New Testament Commentaries (London: Inter-Varsity Press, 2017), 303.

39 Jesus said, "Remove the stone." Martha, the sister of the deceased, said to Him, "Lord, by this time there will be a stench, for he has been [dead] four days." 40 Jesus said to her, "Did I not say to you that if you believe, you will see the glory of God?" 41 So they removed the stone. And Jesus raised His eyes, and said, "Father, I thank You that You have heard Me. 42 "But I knew that You always hear Me; nevertheless, because of the people standing around I said [it,] so that they may believe that You sent Me." 43 And when He had said these things, He cried out with a loud voice, "Lazarus, come out!" 44 Out came the man who had died, bound hand and foot with wrappings, and his face was wrapped around with a cloth. Jesus said to them, "Unbind him, and let him go." [Jhn 11:39-44 NASB20]

This was no ordinary dinner party, but a literal celebration of the greatest miracle ever performed by a family that knew unspeakable joy and gratitude to Christ Jesus for the gift of restored life.

Now, it was known that by Jesus coming so close to Jerusalem that HE was placing HIS life in danger and the Lord Jesus himself had predicted that HE would be crucified by the leaders in Jerusalem.

16 Therefore Thomas, who was called Didymus, said to [his] fellow disciples, "Let's also go, so that we may die with Him!" [Jhn 11:16 NASB20]

22 Jesus said "The Son of Man must suffer many things and be rejected by the elders and chief priests and scribes, and be killed and be raised up on the third day." [Luk 9:22 NASB95]

This gift of bringing Lazarus back from the dead, came with a cost. It would be part of the drama that would lead to Christ Jesus being rejected and slain for the sins of HIS people.   Followed by an even greater resurrection.

Mary, as a disciple of Jesus who loved HIM as her ultimate Prophet, Priest, and Prince, the Messiah of Israel, her Savior, her Lord, her friend, and who had been given the gift of her brother being raised from the dead was moved by the Holy Spirit to provide this extreme gift of honor which would only have been only provided for expressing recognition of one being in the highest ranks of royalty, authority, majesty, worthy of absolute loyalty, admiration, honor, and love by a faithful servant.

Such an anointing normally was saved for a great man at his death in the Jewish culture. A living person as far as we know was never or seldom so honored with such an extravagant expression of adoration, appreciation, and love except for the Lord Jesus Christ.

Even as Mary had seen that the one essential thing was to be sitting at the feet of Jesus being absorbed in HIS presence and taking in HIS words; she also now expresses her recognition that the LORD Jesus is worthy of all honor, praise, and worship.

9 And they sang a new song, saying, "Worthy are You to take the book and to break its seals; for You were slain, and purchased for God with Your blood [men] from every tribe and tongue and people and nation. 10 "You have made them [to be] a kingdom and priests to our God; and they will reign upon the earth." ... 12 saying with a loud voice, "Worthy is the Lamb that was slain to receive

power and riches and wisdom and might and honor and glory and blessing." [Rev 5:9-10, 12 NASB95]

However, Judas has no such vision or feelings toward the Lord Jesus.   To him such an honoring of Jesus Christ was a waste of valuable resources.   Motivated really only by selfish greed he condemns Mary for her act of worship and love.   But not only Judas but the other apostles also see this as a waste according to the gospel of Mark.   This reaction would be what would be expected at such an extravagant and extreme expression of enthusiastic adoration of their Lord.

Only Mary and Jesus seem to really see that this was a good action motivated by love. So many good works to the poor could have been accomplished by this treasure and now they have been wasted on Christ Jesus.

Why such a waste?

Now Judas represents the attitude of total unbelief and hypocritical faith.   He is a double minded man at best and unstable in all of his ways. His focus is selfish, and he has no place in his heart for giving to the Lord Jesus resources, time, or honor unless it would profit himself at the same time.

Watchmen Nee, a church planter in China, gave a message about this event called "Why this Waste". He says this about the attitude of Judas towards Mary.

"That is always the way the world reasons. "Can you not find a better employment for your life? Can you not do something better with yourself than this? It is going a bit too far to give yourself altogether to the Lord!"

But if the Lord is worthy, then how can it be a waste? He is worthy to be so served. He is worthy for me to be His prisoner. He is worthy for me just to live for Him. He is worthy! What the world says about this does not matter.

The Lord says, "Do not trouble her." So let us not be troubled. Men may say what they like, but we can stand on this ground: the Lord said, "It is a good work. Every true work is not done on the poor; every true work is done to Me." When once our eyes have been opened to the real worth of our Lord Jesus, nothing is too good for Him.[26]"

Yet, Judas is able to lead and convince all the other disciples to also be outraged at Mary. Here were men who she respected, apostles of the LORD, preachers, and workers of miracles as they followed the LORD.   These men rebuked her, criticized her, expressed anger at her, and verbally condemned her for expressing her love and adoration in this extreme way.

How do you think she felt at that moment?   Confused, sad, and puzzled?

But the one who defends her, praises her, explains her action perhaps better than she understood, and promises that her act of faith would never be forgotten is the LORD Jesus HIMSELF.

---

[26] Nee, Watchman . Why This Waste? (The Vital Series) . CLC Publications. Kindle Edition.

This should be a warning for us when we are ready to find fault with one of the Lord's servants for not doing things the way we think they should or perhaps for spending so much private time with the LORD.

The truth is that we spend too much time judging others and too little time reflecting on the state of our own hearts before the Lord.

"11 Do not speak against one another, brothers [and sisters.] The one who speaks against a brother [or sister,] or judges his brother [or sister,] speaks against the law and judges the law; but if you judge the law, you are not a doer of the law but a judge [of it.] 12 There is [only] one Lawgiver and Judge, the One who is able to save and to destroy; but who are you, judging your neighbor? "[Jas 4:11-12 NASB20]

As we focus our lives on seeking the "abiding experience" some will judge us for wasting time and not having the right priorities in our lives and service for the Lord. Our desire to do all things in HIS power and as an expression of HIS loving life will seem to lack practicality. Brother Watchmen Nee would call us to keep the most important thing the more important thing.

"There is many a meeting we might address, many a convention at which we might minister, many a gospel campaign in which we might have a share. It is not that we are unable to do it. We could labor and be used to the full, but the Lord is not so concerned about our ceaseless occupation in work for Him. That is not His first object. The service of the Lord is not to be measured by tangible results. No, my friends, the Lord's first concern is with our position at His feet and our anointing of His head. Whatever we have as an "alabaster box"; the most precious thing, the thing dearest in the world to us, yes,—let me say it, the outflow from us of a life that is produced by the very cross itself—we give that all up to the Lord. To some, even of those who should understand, it seems a waste, but that is what He seeks above all. Often enough the giving to Him will be in tireless service, but He reserves to Himself the right to suspend the service for a time in order to make clear to us whether it is that or Himself that holds us.[27]"

We all face the struggle of the issue of Mary and Martha in our lives. Some days we will have the attitude of Mary on the day she was absorbed at Jesus' feet and poured perfume on HIS feet and some days we will be like Mary, who is a disciple, but has become distracted with many things we are doing for the Lord but forgetting the primary importance of our faith relationship with the Lord.

Yet every day, the LORD Jesus loves us and is producing the fruit of love in our lives. Our confidence is never in ourselves to succeed. He as the VINE will produce HIS life in us! That is HIS promise.

17 For the LORD your God is living among you. He is a mighty Savior. HE will take delight in you with gladness. With HIS love, HE will calm all your fears. HE will rejoice over you with joyful songs." [Zep 3:17 NLT]

Prayer

---

[27] Nee, Watchman . Why This Waste? (The Vital Series) . CLC Publications. Kindle Edition

Lord Jesus thank YOU for being the one worthy of all praise, honor, and love. Help me see that spending time with YOU, absorbed by YOU, and aware of YOU is the most important reality of my life. Without YOU I can do nothing and with YOU I will overflow with a wise, sacrificial, and generous life of love. Thank YOU for choosing me to be a branch attached to YOU forever and able to be a means of YOUR LIFE being manifested before the entire universe. Amen

Questions Chapter Fourteen – Day 14

1. Have you ever felt you "wasted" something on the LORD?   When, how, what?

2. Have you ever judged other people for spending too much time praying, journaling, or doing something that you felt was not really the most needed thing at the time? When, how, what?

3. What action in your life would be like pouring out perfume on the Lord?

Personal Journal: I am still growing in really seeing the value of pouring out time, effort, and resources only for the pleasure and praise to be given to the LORD.   There are so many needs and the poor and those hurting will most certainly always be with us providing an opportunity to help them.   Keeping the helping of them as an expression of the Lord Jesus' love for them so that they will love HIM and not just concern for them is vital. Even seeing the LORD Jesus as more important than them is a challenge to me many times.   But this is the key to learning to abide and knowing that only as HIS life overflows out of me to them, do I really do them any good. By making my experience of HIS abiding life and love in me is the only way I really bring any good to anyone for HIS glory and their good.

Chapter Fifteen – The different visions of Jesus I can have to grow in love – Day 15

12 Now we see things imperfectly, like puzzling reflections in a mirror, but then we will see everything with perfect clarity. All that I know now is partial and incomplete, but then I will know everything completely, just as God now knows me completely. [1Co 13:12 NLT]

1 See how very much our Father loves us, for he calls us his children, and that is what we are! But the people who belong to this world don't recognize that we are God's children because they don't know him. 2 Dear friends, we are already God's children, but he has not yet shown us what we will be like when Christ appears. But we do know that we will be like him, for we will see him as he really is. 3 And all who have this eager expectation will keep themselves pure, just as he is pure. [1Jo 3:1-3 NLT]

17 So faith [comes] from hearing, and hearing by the word of Christ. [Rom 10:17 NASB20]

The key prayer we have as we seek a deeper experience of the abiding presence of Christ in us as believers is:

Lord Jesus, let me see YOU more clearly, that I may love YOU more dearly, and follow YOU more nearly day by day. (Richard of Chichester (1197-1253)

Everything depends on seeing the Lord Jesus more clearly one moment at a time by faith. As my vision of HIM grows so will my faith.   But how can I gain a greater vision of Jesus as I see HIS reflection darkly now in a mirror?

I have come to believe we have various "mirrors" through which we can seek a better vision of the Lord Jesus.   They are:

1. The inspired historical gospels of Matthew, Mark, Luke, and John

2. The picture of the exalted Lord Jesus found in the inspired Epistles of the New Testament

3. The unique "Revelation of the Lord Jesus" found in the book of Revelation

4. The perception of the Lord Jesus found in the writings of Moses and the Prophets

5. Church history in its creeds concerning Christ Jesus along with historical events that indicate Jesus Christ interacting and revealing HIMSELF to HIS people

6. Meditation upon world history and nature where it seems the presence of Christ can be seen

7. My personal experiences in which I have felt the presence, peace, and power of Christ Jesus

My development of these "mirrors" was part of a ministry I had for seven years called "Socrates Café" in which the majority of the 20 to 40 people who came were atheists and agnostics. They got to choose the topic we would discuss each month and I would interact with them as a disciple of Jesus. It was one of the best communities that the LORD allowed me to serve during all of these decades of ministry. I had explained to them that the key to my life was having a vision of Jesus that captured my mind and my heart. They doubted if there was enough information about Jesus to bring about such a real devotion. As we talked that afternoon the idea of these seven mirrors of how to develop a relationship with Jesus Christ was developed. They showed appreciation for the answer, surprised that such a complete "vision" of Christ Jesus could be developed. It has been important in my own spiritual growth in faith and deepened my experience of the Life of Christ within me.

Each of these mirrors have to be used carefully. We can wrongly interpret scripture, fail to see errors in church creeds, trust in stories in Church history that we shouldn't, wrongly perceive an event of something in history to be a revelation of Christ, or be mistaken about some part of our personal walk of faith. We must humbly, carefully, and prayerfully do our search to try to be discerning, yet by seeking a greater and greater vision of the Lord Jesus, I believe we can find one and come to love HIM more.

So let us look at each of these "mirrors" and reflect for a moment on each one.

I do recommend the summary of the gospels, epistles, and the Revelation created at bibleproject.com as an aid to get a good overview and introductions to them.   This can help us see Jesus Christ in all of the Scriptures.   I would also recommend the "Life Change" study guides produced by Navpress on all of the books of the Bible as a great way to really deepen your understanding of the witness of Jesus Christ in both the Old and New Testaments. Many of these mirrors will involve some time, effort, and study.

<u>1. The witness of the historic gospels</u>

1 Since many have undertaken to compile an account of the things accomplished among us, 2 just as they were handed down to us by those who from the beginning were eyewitnesses and servants of the word, 3 it seemed fitting to me as well, having investigated everything carefully from the beginning, to write [it out] for you in an orderly sequence, most excellent Theophilus; 4 so that you may know the exact truth about the things you have been taught. [Luk 1:1-4 NASB20]

The gospels give us the most information about God the Son who became the Son of God in the incarnation of Jesus of Nazareth. Here we have real history in true space and time.   The revelation of the Lord Jesus is historical, factual, concrete, and real.   Here we have HIS life and teachings firsthand, presented by those who knew and loved him best.   As can be seen by my use of the gospels in this book I strongly believe that meditation on the events and words of the gospels are critical to our knowing HIM and seeing HIM.

I urge YOU therefore to specifically to take time to read, study, and meditate on Matthew, Mark, Luke, and John seeking a clearer understanding of who Christ Jesus is and what HE has done. This knowledge of the Lord Jesus is foundational to all else we ever come to understand or experience concerning HIM.

I would recommend reading the Diatessaron (160–175 AD) is the most prominent early gospel harmony, and was created by Tatian, an Assyrian early Christian apologist and ascetic. Tatian sought to combine all the textual material he found in the four gospels—Matthew, Mark, Luke, and

John—into a single coherent narrative of Jesus's life and death. This helps to see how all the gospels are really telling one story about one Lord Jesus. I find the reading of it helps me see the unity of the gospels.

2. The Vision of the Lord Jesus in the Epistles

13 For He rescued us from the domain of darkness and transferred us to the kingdom of His beloved Son, 14 in whom we have redemption, the forgiveness of sins. 15 He is the image of the invisible God, the firstborn of all creation: 16 for by Him all things were created, [both] in the heavens and on earth, visible and invisible, whether thrones, or dominions, or rulers, or authorities--all things have been created through Him and for Him. 17 He is before all things, and in Him all things hold together. 18 He is also the head of the body, the church; and He is the beginning, the firstborn from the dead, so that He Himself will come to have first place in everything. 19 For it was the [Father's] good pleasure for all the fullness to dwell in Him, 20 and through Him to reconcile all things to Himself, whether things on earth or things in heaven, having made peace through the blood of His cross. [Col 1:13-20 NASB20]

While the gospels give us a historical vision of who Jesus Christ was in HIS first advent the epistles give us an intellectual and cosmic view of the Lord Jesus as the resurrected, ascended, and glorified Lord. Here we come to understand more fully the meaning of the atoning death of Christ for our sins, the Triune nature of the One God in which the Lord Jesus is "Immanuel" or God with us, our identification with Christ Jesus in HIS death, burial, and resurrection, and HIS new incarnation in the Church which is HIS body. We better understand the eternal and cosmic view of Christ, HIS victory in the resurrection, and how all of the purposes of God will be attained through HIM.

Taking one letter at a time with the purpose of forming a "Christology" from it can be a great benefit in getting a grander and theologically fuller vision of who Jesus Christ has been, is at the present time, and what HE will accomplish in the future.

3. The vision of Jesus in the book of Revelation

1 A great sign appeared in heaven: a woman clothed with the sun, and the moon under her feet, and on her head a crown of twelve stars; 2 and she was pregnant and she cried out, being in labor and in pain to give birth. 3 Then another sign appeared in heaven: and behold, a great red dragon having seven heads and ten horns, and on his heads [were] seven crowns. 4 And his tail swept away a third of the stars of heaven and hurled them to the earth. And the dragon stood before the woman who was about to give birth, so that when she gave birth he might devour her Child. 5 And she gave birth to a Son, a male, who is going to rule all the nations with a rod of iron; and her Child was caught up to God and to His throne. 6 Then the woman fled into the wilderness where she had a place prepared by God, so that there she would be nourished for 1,260 days. [Rev 12:1-6 NASB20]

The book of Revelation is unique in the Bible. It is dedicated to giving us a revelation of who is Christ Jesus. The primary agency of this revelation is through our imagination since this literature is apocalyptic in nature using symbols and pictures to convey truth. This vivid use of language opens up fresh visions of who is Jesus Christ and forms emotional insights that could not be attained in any other way of revelation. I believe that a careful meditation on the various visions given to John in the Revelation can help us respond to Christ Jesus in a powerful way and increase our hope in HIS redemptive return to bring back Eden on steroids.

4. The understanding of Moses and the Prophets vision of Christ Jesus the Messiah of Israel

1 Why are the nations restless And the peoples plotting in vain? 2 The kings of the earth take their stand And the rulers conspire together Against the LORD and against His Anointed, [saying,] 3 "Let's tear their shackles apart And throw their ropes away from us!" 4 He who sits in the heavens laughs, The Lord scoffs at them. 5 Then He will speak to them in His anger And terrify them in His fury, [saying,] 6 "But as for Me, I have installed My King Upon Zion, My holy mountain." 7 "I will announce the decree of the LORD: He said to Me, 'You are My Son, Today I have fathered You. 8 'Ask [it] of Me, and I will certainly give the nations as Your inheritance, And the ends of the earth as Your possession. 9 'You shall break them with a rod of iron, You shall shatter them like earthenware.'" 10 Now then, you kings, use insight; Let yourselves be instructed, you judges of the earth. 11 Serve the LORD with reverence And rejoice with trembling. 12 Kiss the Son, that He not be angry and you perish [on] the way, For His wrath may be kindled quickly. How blessed are all who take refuge in Him! [Psa 2:1-12 NASB20]

This is a prophetic vision of Christ Jesus that was given since the earliest of times with the promise of an anointed Savior and King that would restore the Kingdom of God fully to the earth and overcome the curse brought to the earth due to rebellion and sin. Knowledge of these prophecies is assumed by the New Testament authors and is reflected in the majority of the verses found in the book of Revelation. Catching the images, predictions, and promises of the coming "Messiah" or Christ gives a much fuller understanding of who is Jesus Christ, creating the context of the promises given before HE was conceived.

I recommend the book <u>All the Messianic Prophecies of the Bible</u> by Herbert Lockyer as a great way to start a study, meditation, and search to understand the hundreds of prophecies that predicted the person and work of Christ Jesus since the beginning of human history. Part of our confidence and trust in Jesus of Nazareth being the 'Chosen One" is because of his fulfillment of all these prophetic promises.

5. Finding a Vision of Christ in the Creeds and History of the Church

18 "And I also say to you that you are Peter, and upon this rock I will build My church; and the gates of Hades will not overpower it. [Mat 16:18 NASB20]

1 In my first book I told you, Theophilus, about everything Jesus began to do and teach 2 until the day he was taken up to heaven after giving his chosen apostles further instructions through the Holy Spirit. 3 During the forty days after his crucifixion, he appeared to the apostles from time to the Kingdom of God. 4 Once when he was eating with them, he commanded them, "Do not leave Jerusalem until the Father sends you the gift he promised, as I told you before. [Act 1:1-4 NLT]

19 Therefore, go and make disciples of all the nations, baptizing them in the name of the Father and the Son and the Holy Spirit. 20 Teach these new disciples to obey all the commands I have given you. And be sure of this: I am with you always, even to the end of the age." [Mat 28:19-20 NLT]

15 Let the peace of Christ, to which you were indeed called in one body, rule in your hearts; and be thankful. [Col 3:15 NASB20]

It is important that we see that the abiding life of Christ has been filling believers for two thousand years. Beginning in the book of Acts where Luke says that Jesus Christ is continuing to do and teach through HIS body of disciples till the present time, the Church or "Community of the King" has existed, witnessed to the gospel, demonstrated the love of the Holy Spirit, and manifested the power of the Holy Spirit throughout history.   The assembly of believers have become the primary educators of the human race, given more to help the needy than any other human institution, and at their best brought critical social reforms to dark pagan nations.

There are libraries of books of prayer, meditations on spiritual issues, and commentaries without number on every book of the Bible from a Christ Centered perspective. We are standing on the shoulders of giants of the faith both in their intellect and lives. We have a rich and overflowing heritage of faith if we begin to look at it with discerning minds and hearts.

There is much we can learn from the generations of believers who have sought to serve, know, and bear fruit for Christ Jesus over the last two millenniums. Some of the best minds and most noble souls in human history have been "branches of the Vine" and sources of insight and compassion.

There have been dark hours also in which those who claimed to know the Lord Jesus represented more of the spirit of "Anti-Christ" and plagued history with false doctrine and immoral lives. The letters to the churches in the book of Revelation would indicate that 70% of the first century congregations were struggling to live in a way worthy of the gospel and were called by Christ Jesus to repent. But this fact did not mean that the Church community was a failure.

There always have been a true remanent of true overcoming believers who have taught and lived the Life of Christ in a true way before the watching world. Imperfectly to be sure, but in a substantial way they bore the fruit of love and truth before their generation. From this great host of witnesses, we can learn and also be warned by those who failed to successfully follow the Lord, least we repeat their errors.

In the positive expression of faith and life by billions of Christians over two thousand years we can see the life of Christ bearing fruit through HIS branches. Our goal in looking at Church History is to see past the weakness of believers to see the abundant life of the Living Christ shining through.

Our secular culture has a very negative perspective on the Church and has had a tendency to ignore the evidence of the love of Christ found in the community of faith and only put emphasis on the hypocrisy and abuse one can find in some parts of professing Christianity. But Jesus has promised HE would build HIS community of disciples and the gates of hell would never overcome this witness of HIS life and love. We should reject this overly negative view of the Church and seek to see in the body of believers the presence, power, and peace of the LORD Jesus.

One example of this was how Christians showed mercy to sick people during plagues.

"As sociologist Rodney Stark noted in <u>The Triumph of Christianity: How the Jesus Movement Became the World's Largest Religion</u>, Christians responded to the plagues differently than their pagan neighbors.

"During the first plague, the famous classical physician Galen fled Rome for his country estate where he stayed until the danger subsided. But for those who could not flee, the typical response was to try to avoid any contact with the afflicted, since it was understood that the disease was contagious. Hence, when their first symptom appeared, victims often were thrown into the streets, where the dead and dying lay in piles," Stark wrote.

Bishop Dionysius recounted the events in Alexandria, Egypt, during the Cyprian Plague: "At the first onset of the disease, they [pagans] pushed the sufferers away and fled from their dearest, throwing them into the roads before they were dead and treated unburied corpses as dirt, hoping thereby to avert the spread and contagion of the fatal disease."

Yet Christians sought to help the sick, even risking their own lives. As Cyprian, bishop of Carthage, put it, "Although this mortality had contributed nothing else, it has especially accomplished this for Christians and servants of God, that we have begun gladly to seek martyrdom while we are learning not to fear death."[28]

It was the Christian Church that formed the first hospitals and provided medical care to the ancient world.

"As a means of caring for those who were ill, St. Basil of Caesarea founded the first hospital (c. 369). Christian hospitals grew apace, spreading throughout both the East and the West. By the mid-1500s there were 37,000 Benedictine monasteries alone that cared for the sick.[29]

Not only were to bodies of people shown the LOVE of Christ through these hospitals but the gospel of Christ was shared as well. Both body, soul, and spirit were helped by the compassion and mercy of Christ overflowing from the believers who started these houses of healing. These are just two of thousands of examples of the Life of Christ being seen in sacrificial acts of love due to faith in Jesus Christ over two millenniums.

Ask the Holy Spirit to open your eyes to not only see the presence of Christ living in the history of believers in the past but also in followers of the Lord Jesus that impacted your life. Focus not on those who have disappointed you or hurt you, but instead on those "branches of the VINE" that showed YOU the Love of Christ, and helped YOU believe. Seeing the presence of Christ in each other is a vital way we can become aware of the "abiding" life of the LORD in our midst. We are after all HIS BODY now manifested on the earth.

A couple of books that may help you gain insight into seeing the presence of Christ Jesus manifested in HIS people are, <u>What If Jesus Had Never Been Born?</u> by DR. D James Kennedy and Jerry Newcombe and <u>Church History in Plain Language</u> by Bruce Shelley. Seeing how Christ has impacted all of history through HIS people in positive ways can help us also see how HE is active today in HIS people and in our own lives.

---

[28] https://pjmedia.com/culture/tyler-o-neil/2020/03/17/how-early-christians-saved-lives-and-spread-the-gospel-during-roman-plagues-n379331

[29] https://biblemesh.com/blog/the-christian-origins-of-hospitals/

6. Seeing the Presence of Christ in nature and world events

1 For the music director. A Psalm of David. The heavens tell of the glory of God; And their expanse declares the work of His hands. 2 Day to day pours forth speech, And night to night reveals knowledge. 3 There is no speech, nor are there words; Their voice is not heard. 4 Their line has gone out into all the earth, And their words to the end of the world. In them He has placed a tent for the sun, 5 Which is like a groom coming out of his chamber; It rejoices like a strong person to run his course. 6 Its rising is from one end of the heavens, And its circuit to the other end of them; And there is nothing hidden from its heat. [Psa 19:1-6 NASB20]

1 Nebuchadnezzar the king to all the peoples, nations, and [populations of all] languages who live in all the earth: "May your peace be great! 2 "I am pleased to declare the signs and miracles that the Most High God has done for me. 3 "How great are His signs And how mighty are His miracles! His kingdom is an everlasting kingdom, And His dominion is from generation to generation. ... 37 "Now I, Nebuchadnezzar, praise, exalt, and honor the King of heaven, for all His works are true and His ways just; and He is able to humble those who walk in pride." [Dan 4:1-3, 37 NASB20]

It is not only in the history of the Church that we can see the wonder of the Living Christ but also in the wonder of the Created World. Since Christ is the creator of all of nature taking time to study and meditate on the order, beauty, and power of nature can cause us to have an increased vision of the wisdom and abilities of our Savior and LORD. [30]

One book and movie that I find inspiring and helps me appreciate Christ as Creator is The Privileged Planet which points out contrary to popular belief, Earth is not an insignificant blip on the universe's radar. Our world proves anything but average in Guillermo Gonzalez and Jay W. Richards' The Privileged Planet: How Our Place in the Cosmos Is Designed for Discovery. But what exactly does Earth bring to the table? How does it prove its worth among numerous planets and constellations in the vastness of the Milky Way? In The Privileged Planet, you'll learn about the earth's:

life-sustaining capabilities

water and its miraculous makeup

protection by the planetary giants

And how our planet came into existence in the first place.

Such studies help us to be in awe of Christ Jesus as the mind and wisdom of such a great Cosmos and that there are good intellectual reasons to see HIS intelligence as the one that designed our universe. Such a study can help us really appreciate the Cosmic Christ that is living in our hearts.[31]

---

[30] Books that can help to increase our vision of Jesus Christ as the brilliant and wise Creator can be found in Intelligent Design: The Bridge Between Science and Theology by William A. Dembski and Michael Behe.

[31] You can learn more about the Privileged Planet at https://privilegedplanet.com/
You can watch the movie by going to: https://go2rpi.com/privileged-planet-video-on-demand/

In addition, we can begin reading history as "HIS STORY" and look for Christ Jesus' presence in the tangled mess of a rebellious world. Since all good things are gifts from HIM to HIS creation beginning to see HIM at work in the middle of a troubled world can give us a different awareness of the cosmic nature of our Lord and Savior.

One example of this can be found in the "Miracle of Dunkirk" in World War II. The story is summarized by Peter Grieg in his wonderful book <u>How to Pray; A guide for ordinary people</u>.

"One of the most dramatic examples of the power of united intercession in modern times took place in May 1940, as the Second World War was entering its darkest and most dangerous chapter. The Allied forces were trapped by the advancing Nazi forces with their backs to the sea at Dunkirk. The German High Command had announced that its troops were proceeding to annihilate the British army, Winston Churchill was preparing to admit an unprecedented military catastrophe, and Allied generals were secretly anticipating the loss of a third of a million soldiers.

In utter despair, King George VI took to the airwaves on Thursday, May 23, 1940, calling the people of Great Britain to a National Day of Prayer the following Sunday. Old black-and-white photographs show somber crowds that Sunday, waiting to get into cathedrals, churches, and chapels, an entire nation united in seeking God for national deliverance. The very next day, a flotilla of some 860 vessels—mostly civilian craft—set out to cross the English Channel in a desperate, ramshackle attempt to rescue besieged Allied soldiers. Churchill hoped that as many as 30,000 men, 10 percent of the beleaguered army, could be rescued.

By the time the ships reached France, they were highly vulnerable to aerial attack. So, too, was the Allied army amassed like a sitting target on the beach at Dunkirk. But unseasonal storms blew up, battering the European mainland so violently that the Luftwaffe in that region was grounded, unable to attack. Meanwhile, Hitler had inexplicably ordered his ground forces to halt. For three days, they didn't move. His generals were furious, and military historians to this day are still baffled by this clear tactical error. And so, with the Luftwaffe grounded by an unexpected storm and the German army restrained by its own commander, the Dunkirk evacuations were allowed to proceed largely undisrupted until the Luftwaffe resumed their attacks on May 29.

On Wednesday, three days after the National Day of Prayer, and in sharp contrast to the storms of the previous day, an extraordinary calm descended on the English Channel, precisely the benign conditions that the overloaded boats now needed as they sailed back to England. By the time that the German army finally renewed its attack, more than 338,000 men had been rescued, ten times the expected number, including 140,000 French, Belgian, Dutch, and Polish soldiers.

No wonder the events of those remarkable days became known as "the Miracle of Dunkirk." In his famous speech to Parliament on June 4, 1940, Churchill heralded "a miracle of deliverance." A second Day of Prayer was called to thank God for delivering a third of a million lives, confounding the plans of the enemy, and redirecting the entire trajectory of the Second World War. We must be very careful indeed about claiming God's partisan support or overt blessing in any theater of war. But it is without doubt that a series of critical elements in the success of the Dunkirk evacuations lay so far beyond the hand of the Allied powers that they must either be labeled as luck on a quite extraordinary scale or as answers to the unprecedented, concerted prayers of an entire nation that ascended to heaven on the day that it all began."[32]

It should be noted that the vast majority of these prayers were made in the name and authority of Christ Jesus and to the Triune God of the Scriptures. Here people were crying out to for this great deliverance which was a key to the eventual saving of over a quarter of million lives and "a miracle" occurred.

While we may be limited in our ability to aways make sense of history as "HIS STORY" we can begin to ask for wisdom about how to do this and to seek out examples of the LORD Jesus being active in the affairs of humanity. He has promised that all things are going to work out for good for HIS people and HIS kingdom eventually.   The more we can detect this truth, the more we can have our faith in HIM increase.

7. Gaining A Vision of Christ Jesus by mapping out YOUR own faith walk with HIM

5 Test yourselves [to see] if you are in the faith; examine yourselves! Or do you not recognize [this about] yourselves, that Jesus Christ is in you--unless indeed you fail the test? [2Co 13:5 NASB20]

This is really a spiritual exercise that may take you some time but is one of the most important in this book as you seek to learn to enjoy the abiding presence of Christ in your life.

Imagine your life is a "Gospel". This is the "Gospel of (Your Name).

Separate your life into chapters.   Some of the chapter should be seen as before YOU met Jesus Christ in a personal way.   For some of us this may be hard since we were raised in Christian homes and always had some knowledge of Jesus Christ.   For others there will be a very sharp division of before and after. Still for others we may feel we once had a great relationship with the Lord and then found ourselves feeling disconnected or even denying, now followed by a present season of faith.   There are no right ways to do this, just be honest.

Write about your relationship with Jesus Christ as you have experienced it.

The divisions are whatever seems meaningful to you.

Under each section, set aside the most significant events both positive and negative.

1) What events or people hurt you, hindered you, or abused you? Who made it hard for you to trust in Christ Jesus.
2) What have you done that hurt, hindered, or abused others making it hard for them to know Jesus Christ?

---

[32] Greig, Pete. How to Pray: A Simple Guide for Normal People (pp. 107-108). The Navigators. Kindle Edition.

3) What events or people helped you, gave you pleasure, provided you peace, did a good deed to support you, encouraged you or blessed you? How did these events or people help YOU see the Love of Jesus for YOU?
4) Is there a moment or moments when YOU believe that Jesus Christ began to abide in YOU and YOU had true abiding faith in HIM. How, why, and when did this occur?
5) What have you done that helped, supported, did good for the benefit of other people or for Jesus Christ?
6) Were there times when you felt Jesus Christ disappointed you, failed you, cursed you or condemned you?
7) Were there times when you felt the life of Jesus Christ in you, saved you, delivered you, answered your prayers, or gave you strength to get through a hard time?
8) Other important things that happened but don't seem to fit under these circumstances that would be important to put in your "Gospel".

Give each "chapter" of your "Gospel" a title.

After you have worked through your life up to the present, give your entire "Gospel" a title.

Also, summarize under each section any "life rules", "personal proverbs", "vows", or "life lessons" that came about because of a particular incident. Record any particular revelations or insights about Christ Jesus that you have gained up to this point in YOUR life in your experience.

As you look at these "life principles" and "revelations about Jesus", ask yourself if you are satisfied this represents the values and operating systems that Jesus would want in your life?

Would you be happy if your children or those most precious to you lived their lives by these precepts and beliefs? Why or why not?

Is Jesus Christ asking to repent of some of your personal convictions about life?

Also, take each of the significant events and write your thoughts, feelings, questions, and musings about it with a special focus on detecting the presence, peace, and power of Jesus Christ.

Write about the event until you have nothing left in you to write about it.

Write letters in your journal to those who hurt you. You can express your anger, hurt, disappointment, and confusion. But chose to forgive them even as Christ Jesus forgave you.

Do you need to write a letter to someone that you have injured their faith in Jesus Christ? Are there things to need to "cast on HIM because HE cares for you"? (1 Peter 5:7)

I know this is a big spiritual assignment, but I have found this exercise worth doing in my life several times. Each time I do this process of "remembering" I gain some new insights into how the LORD Jesus has been active in my life and is changing me to become more and more a channel of HIS love into the world.

May the LORD allow this exercise to do the same in your life.

The Big Idea

17 So faith [comes] from hearing, and hearing by the word of Christ. [Rom 10:17 NASB20]

The "Big Idea" of this chapter has been to encourage you to grow in your vision of Christ Jesus so that your love for Christ Jesus may increase and YOUR awareness of HIS abiding presence in you, around you, over you, and under you may be felt and that HIS life of love will overflow more and more out of your life.

The greater our vision of Christ the greater our faith and the greater our faith the more abundant our fruit will be in all of life.

Prayer: Lord I need to see YOU more clearly, my vision of YOU is very limited, help me seek and hunger after a greater and greater vision of WHO YOU are, what YOU are doing, and how trustworthy YOU are in YOUR character, competence, and compassion. LORD, increase my faith by increasing my vision of YOU at work in me, around me, above me, under me, and surrounding me. Overflow YOUR abiding life through me today that YOU may be seen great, good, and full of grace! Amen

Journal for Chapter Fifteen – Day 15

1. Which of the mirrors do you find most useful in giving you a vision of Christ Jesus' abiding presence in YOUR life? Why?

2. Which of the mirrors would you find most difficult to ever apply?   Why?

3. What one concrete action could you take to seek a clearer vision of Jesus Christ?

Personal Journal – At different times in my life different "mirrors" have served to increase my vison and love for Jesus Christ in my life.   The writing and reflecting on "The Gospel According To Norm" has done more than anything else for me to grow in my faith at a practical level. Focusing on the experience I personally have had with the living Christ makes it very hard for me to deny the reality of HIS involvement in my life.   I have also been helped by meditation, study, and reading of the gospels and especially the resurrection accounts that for me "seal the deal" that Christ Jesus is the only place to go to find "eternal life" which is a fellowship with the divine. So for me these are at the moment the most significance "mirror images" of Jesus that give me faith daily.

I hope you have found the reading, praying, meditating, and journaling of this book helpful in your "abiding experience".

A final Word – Chapter Sixteen.

Thank you for joining me in this desire to find a way to better engage in our sojourn with Christ in our lives of daily faith. I appreciate your participation in this process of better experiencing the Living presence of Christ.   As I stated at the beginning this is not really a book to be read but more of a spiritual process to be done over a period of time to awaken us to the reality of the Living Christ bearing fruit, change, and practical expressions of HIS love into our lives. I hope you have approached that way seeking the Holy Spirit's help in deepening YOUR vision of our Lord Jesus Christ.

To get the most from the book I would go over each day again reviewing and deepening what you got the first time around. Yes, that means that it will take a whole month to really process the entire book carefully and prayerfully. But I wrote this book to actually be used by the LORD to become a doorway for you to grow in YOUR faith connection with HIM and become abundant in fulfilling HIS will for your life which is to overflow with the fruit of practical expressions of love for HIM and others. With that goal in mind, I think it is a good investment of your time and focus and hope you will take up the challenge.

There is a lot of intentional "spaced repetition" in the book because it has been shown that the emotional aspect of our minds only is really converted by ritual and repetition so that not only our logical mind, but emotional mind can be converted. The hope and prayer is your heart as well as your head has been reached with the need of experiencing the reality of our abiding in Christ.

First thing to do today is to just scan each chapter looking for what was the most important ideas and experiences you had from each chapter.   Summarize them here and if you have experienced any spiritual events or changed any behaviors make note of them here for your review.

My sincere prayer is that this book will be used to open the eyes of your heart to see the greatness and glory of Christ's love for you. Amen

14 For this reason I bend my knees before the Father, 15 from whom every family in heaven and on earth derives its name, 16 that He would grant you, according to the riches of His glory, to be strengthened with power through His Spirit in the inner self, 17 so that Christ may dwell in your hearts through faith; [and] that you, being rooted and grounded in love, 18 may be able to comprehend with all the saints what is the width and length and height and depth, 19 and to know the love of Christ which surpasses knowledge, that you may be filled to all the fullness of God. 20 Now to Him who is able to do far more abundantly beyond all that we ask or think, according to the power that works within us, 21 to Him [be] the glory in the church and in Christ Jesus to all generations forever and ever. Amen. [Eph 3:14-21 NASB20]

Journal For Chapter 16 – Summarize the main things you gained from reading the book

Make the subject: My thoughts about The One Essential Thing

<u>Closing Serenity Prayer</u>

Heavenly Father, grant me the serenity
to accept the things I cannot change;
courage to change the things I can;
and wisdom to know the difference.
Living one day at a time;
enjoying one moment at a time;
accepting hardships as the pathway to peace;
taking, as my LORD Jesus did, this sinful world
as it is, not as I would have it;
trusting that the LORD Jesus will make all things work together for good
if I by faith abide in HIS LOVE and have HIS Life flow out of me;
that I may be reasonably happy in this life
and supremely happy with Him
forever in the next.
Amen.

Disclaimer: The only book I fully endorse is the bible and so while I found these books and videos to be very helpful in my growth, I am not saying they should be read without a careful and prayerful consideration of what they say and always tested by the Scriptures. However, I believe that the authors of these books and videos had important insights and revelations that aided me in my own growth in grace. So just as sermons are part of God's plan to help us grow so also books and videos by other believers can help us to be built up in our faith and understanding.   So read and watch them with a desire to grow, a discerning mind and open heart.

1. <u>True Spirituality</u> by Francis Schaeffer – This book was the first one that caused me to see that the gospel of the death, burial, and resurrection was not just to get forgiven but to be the focus of my entire Christian life.

2. <u>The Normal Christian Life</u> by Watchmen Nee – This book was given to me by my spiritual mentor Jerry Mobley and echoed many of the insights coming from Dr. Schaeffer's book. Nee is Chinese and so his perspective is different but refreshing.   The illustrations he uses really helped me get a better heart vision of living by the gospel and seeing myself in union and communion with Christ.

3. <u>Abiding In Christ</u> by Andrew Murray – A devotional focused on this union and communion with Christ that helped me stay with this focus over a month. Helpful for keeping my heart focused on being in connection with Jesus.

4. <u>Life Change Study Guide on the gospel of John</u> by the Navigators. – This book allows you to carefully and prayerfully study the gospel of John to gain a better knowledge of who Jesus is and what HE has done. This can be done individually or in a group. Great resource.

5. Pocket Testament League has a 21-day online guide to the gospel of John. Google 21-day challenge by Pocket Testament League.

6. <u>A Journal of Sacred Reading</u> by Ken Boa – I learned how to do sacred reading at a men's retreat in which the main speaker was Ken Boa. This book is a very practical book that allows you to do sacred readings on selected passages and grow in encountering the presence, power, and peace of Jesus in the Scriptures. It has had a great impact on me.

7. <u>Counterfeit Gods: The Empty Promises of Money, Sex, and Power, and the Only Hope that Matters</u> by Tim Keller – Tim Keller has some of the most profound insights on the issue of how we struggle still today in our modern culture with idols of the heart.

8. Sermon by Dr. Lockridge "That's My King". Google "That's my King" by Dr. Lockridge to hear a recording of the message. Very inspiring and speaks to the heart to really want to personally "Know Jesus".   This has become one of my favorite devotional messages.

9. <u>Search For Significance</u> by Robert McGee – This book was a life changing experience in which not only my mind but my emotions were really converted to trust that God in Christ wildly accepted me and loved me.   The journaling part of the book is vital and is in the back. This is a "must read and do" book in my thinking for everyone wanting to live a life of consistent faith.

10. <u>Prayer: Finding the Hearts True Home</u> by Richard Foster – I read this book on a vacation while traveling by train. It was a book that renewed my focus on prayer and had a huge impact on my understanding of spiritual warfare.

11. <u>The Plan of Salvation</u> – by B.B. Warfield.   This book was the most important book I read during my years in seminary.   This book is for the mind and not primarily for the heart, but it allows us to really try to understand how God planned our salvation from beginning to end.   A short book but rich in content.

12. <u>Walking With God through Pain and Suffering</u> – by Tim Keller – This book is the best book dealing with the reality of pain and suffering here "East of Eden" that I have read combining intellectual, emotion, philosophical, and pastoral insights and wonderful stories of people who have walked by faith through very hard times.

13. <u>The Problem of Pain </u>by C.S. Lewis – A classic discussion on the philosophical answers we can have to knowing that we can trust God in Christ to be good, great, and full of grace in the midst of a world that has pain and evil.   The movie "Shadowland" is an important balance to this book since it deals with how he handled the loss of his wife to cancer.

14. <u>How to Pray: A Simple Guide</u> by Pete Greig is really the best practical book on prayer that I have read and really can help us know how to develop an in-depth experience of our abiding relationship with Jesus Christ.   Also google his "Prayer Course One" and Prayer Course Two" along with the 24/7 prayer movement for many more good resources

15. <u>Sacred Pathways</u> by Gary Thomas was another book I read while on vacation at my timeshare on the beach.   This book opened me up to the reality of how different each of us can be in our journey with God and also that sometimes I need to try a different style when my experience of the abiding relationship with Christ has seemed to dry up.

16. Google – "Learning How To Lament" – Vineyard Church for a guide on how to lament.

17. Why This Waste by Watchman Nee – This book opened my heart to not just doing things but doing them "for Jesus alone". Great message.

18. Google to watch the video – "The Privileged Planet" to begin to see the wisdom of Jesus in how he created the universe.

19. Google the "Serenity Prayer" by the Skit Guys for a short but profound insight into this prayer.

20. Go to the "Bibleproject.com for many good resources on understanding the scriptures

Appendix: Orchid: A Story of Attachment

by Kat Silverglate, Founder of The Ridiculous Hour Foundation,
www.theridiculoushour.com

I really couldn't be mad. By every visible measure, the thing had been dead for ages. It wasn't a sudden death either. More a slow fade I fought valiantly to prevent. A gift from my firm during a medical challenge, it arrived in a spectacular vessel. The florist had carved a well in the body of a tree trunk section leaving the outside bark largely intact. The hollowed center, just big enough to house the intricate root structure, was covered in Spanish moss.

The day it arrived, the leaves were so plump; they stood vertically above the container's edge with no support. Angel white blooms the size of mature sand dollars were so heavy that wood rods and clips kept them from topplingover.

It wasn't just an extraordinary gift. It was God's living art.

Knowing nothing about the care and feeding of an orchid, I treated it like one might a vase of fresh cut flowers: lots of water; a spot in the center of the dining room table; and, little regard for time in direct sunlight. When the wilted blooms started to dot the table like jumbo confetti and the leaves decided to permanently recline after turning a jaundiced yellow, I tried everything to save it.

Less water.
More sun.
Pruning.
Pep talks.
Springsteen.

Nothing worked. Sentimentally attached and definitely not ready to admit defeat (even after it shrunk by half to a brittle brown root ball) I decided to move it to the furthest corner of the pool deck where I hoped it would one day come miraculously to life. By the time spring cleaning came around, it was difficult to be angry when the orchid, trunk and all, got swept up and thrown in the trash.

Here's what I would come to learn about orchids. I wish I remembered who taught me this so I could give attribution here, but I don't. All I know is this tiny tutorial changed the way I see just about everything that appears to be hopeless. If you tie the roots of an orchid to a living tree with burlap - or some other material that allows water to flow through the roots - it will come alive as long as the roots attach to the bark. Sounds odd, I know, but it works! At least in a tropical environment.

I tested it by pulling every dying orchid I could find from trash heaps and by convincing friends to give me their dead
plants.

After tying a fair number of "dead" orchids to live trees, I can say this with some conviction:"It's pretty darn hard to find a dead orchid. No matter how far gone it seems, attach those roots to a living tree and see what happens."
Look at these images:

Those are from the tree in our front yard loaded with orchids. Not only do the roots gain what they need from the tree, they have become so attached that the bark and the roots seem almost one. In many spots, the roots are now hidden in the folds of the tree bark. The transformation that attachment brings is remarkable to witness.

"Remain in me," the Lord says, "as I also remain in you. No branch can bear fruit by itself; it must remain in the vine. Neither can you bear fruit unless you remain in me. I am the vine; you are the branches. If you remain in me and I in you, you will bear much fruit; apart from me you can do nothing."
John 15:4-5.

God says attach. Attach to the source of life. Like the branch to the vine. Like the orchid to the tree. And remain.

If ever there was a cultural moment to do an attachment inventory, now seems to be ideal. To what are we attaching as we seek renewal? Hope? By just about every criteria - financial, political, environmental, social - challenges abound. For many, substantial segments of life feel as brittle and dry as the trashed orchid. We reach for important things to refresh and help us -- nutrition, exercise, medical attention, therapy. Awesome! In our attachment inventory, how might we describe our "remain in me" moments?

If you'd like to try a 30 spiritual practice that encourages healthy attachment, visit The Ridiculous Hour's Mission page at

www.theridiculoushour.com/mobile-mission
and search for the June 2022 Mission
titled Orchid.

You can hear the podcast or read the blog with the spiritual practice activity at the bottom of the post. Or, you can receive a copy of the mission activity in your mailbox by emailing

kat@theridiculoushour.com

I highly recommend you get the monthly spiritual assignments from "The Ridiculous hour".
They are an important part of my spiritual nourishment.